"Evangelicals who believe that 'politics is a dirty business but somebody else needs to do it' should think twice. Politics is God's business and evangelicals need to do it. Bob Dugan tells us why and how in a book that's not only easy to read but important to practice."

Dr. Haddon Robinson, *President, Denver Seminary*

"Every Christian is accountable to God to be a good citizen and that means being involved in the political processes. Robert Dugan writes with great personal insight and experience about our American political process and how much influence Christians can really have. This book is a must for anyone who wants to make a real difference!"

Bill Bright, *President, Campus Crusade for Christ International*

"Now we know why Bob Dugan has won the respect of Washington with a sane and sound voice for evangelical Christians. He practices what he preaches in this book— doing his homework, daring to speak, depending on God, and never giving up hope—the art of Christian action in politics. A fast-moving, hard-hitting guide for all of us."

David L. McKenna, *President, Asbury Theological Seminary*

"With the goal of mobilizing evangelical America to rise to the current challenge, Bob Dugan has written a book that is inspiring and highly accessible to the layman who senses a need to get involved in politics. The work is part nuts-and-bolts political textbook and part theological foundation for such activity. In addition, Dugan's book is courageous, unwilling to accept the easy answers and half-efforts some Christians use to rationalize their lacking political interest."

Mark O. Hatfield, *United States Senator*

"Bob Dugan combines experience in politics with evangelical perspective to help us see through the political fog and to tell us in practical steps how to change America for good. I know of no other book that does the job so well."

Leith Anderson, *Pastor, Wooddale Church, Eden Prairie, MN.*

"A resounding trumpet call to carefully nuanced evangelical political engagement amid America's present moral crisis."

Carl F. H. Henry, *evangelical theologian and author*

Winning
the New
Civil
War

WINNING THE NEW CIVIL WAR

RECAPTURING AMERICA'S VALUES

ROBERT P. DUGAN, JR.

FOREWORD
SENATOR WILLIAM L. ARMSTRONG

MULTNOMAH

Portland, Oregon 97266

To contact the National Association of Evangelicals, write or call:

National Association of Evangelicals
450 Gundersen Drive
Carol Stream, IL 60188
(708) 665-0500

NAE Office of Public Affairs
1023 15th Street NW, Suite 500
Washington, DC 20005
(202) 789-1011

Unless otherwise indicated, all Scripture references are from the Holy Bible: New International Version, copyright 1973, 1978, 1984 by the International Bible Society. Used by permission of Zondervan Bible Publishers.

Cover design by Durand Demlow.

WINNING THE NEW CIVIL WAR
©1991 by Robert P. Dugan Jr.
Published by Multnomah Press
10209 SE Division Street
Portland, Oregon 97266

Multnomah Press is a ministry of Multnomah School of the Bible, 8435 NE Glisan Street, Portland, Oregon 97220.

Printed in the United States of America.

Library of Congress Cataloging in Publication Data

Dugan, Robert P.
   Winning the new civil war : recapturing America's values
/ Robert P. Dugan, Jr.
   Includes bibliographical references
   ISBN 0-88070-408-X
   1. Christianity and politics. 2. United States—Politics and government. I. Title.
BR115.P7D79 1991
261.7'0973—dc20
                                   90-22664
                                          CIP

92 93 94 95 96 97 98 99 00 - 10 9 8 7 6 5 4 3

Dedication

To the people who mean everything to me

Lynne
who has loved and supported me without reservation for
over thirty-seven years whether in
pastoral ministry or unsuccessful run for Congress

Bob and Cheri
who honor their father and mother
and whose future motivated me to write this book

Robert P. and Marion S. Dugan
who, by teaching and example, have passed on to me
the priceless heritage of the Christian faith

Contents

Acknowledgments

For the better part of a decade, Brenda Jose of Multnomah Press quietly urged me to undertake a book. Even though I had written many an article and, through 1990, 142 *NAE Washington Insight* newsletters, the prospect of authoring a book had always seemed too daunting a task. Without Brenda's well-timed encouragements, backed by the assurances of publisher John Van Diest, this book would not have been added to the collection anticipated in Ecclesiastes 12:12. I could not be more grateful to them.

Steve Halliday must have drawn the short straw, because he was assigned to be my editor. It was his lot to explain to this first-time author that the original manuscript was not perfect. Steve did that with sufficient grace that, together, we sharpened the book's focus, following which he edited with skill and wisdom. Any editor who in turn can tolerate the author editing his editing, deserves praise.

I have no greater respect and admiration for any national leader than for United States Senator William L. Armstrong of Colorado. He understands full well the culture war in which our nation is engaged, and has courageously championed traditional values in battle after battle. I am honored that he consented to write the Foreword for this book.

While this book was written evenings and weekends, rather than on company time, I nonetheless pay tribute to a group of competent professional colleagues in NAE's Washington office: Richard Cizik, Tim Crater, Forest Montgomery, Brian O'Connell, and Curran Tiffany, with my assistant Jodie Koan keeping things humming as office manager. Over the years, each has played a significant role in honing my thinking and battling for common convictions.

Foreword

Bob Dugan would have made a great Congressman. He's smart, energetic, meets people well, and has a voice that resonates with authority. He is also an excellent public speaker with a flair for clearly and persuasively stating his case on complex issues of public policy.

So it was only natural that Bob would run for office. And in 1976 he did so, becoming a candidate for the United States House of Representatives. Had he won the election, it could have been the start of a brilliant political career.

But this book might never have been written.

Thoughtful Christians, especially those of us who are alarmed about the moral depravity of our days, have good reason to be thankful this book was written. Let us hope that it will be widely read and acted upon by believers everywhere.

It turned out that the Lord did not plan for Bob to become a Congressman, at least not in 1976. Instead Bob was called to the nation's capital to head the Office of Public Affairs of the National Association of Evangelicals. In that capacity, he has become one of America's leading strategists and spokesmen on moral, legislative, and political issues of concern to Christians.

Most of us, especially followers of Jesus Christ, *are*

concerned. We realize that America, despite its greatness and freedom and prosperity, is deeply troubled. Thoughtful citizens can scarcely ignore the grisly toll that suicide, abortion, divorce, drugs, pornography, homosexuality, secularism, cheating, and cynicism have had on our beloved country.

Our Lord asked, "What will a man be profited if he gains the whole world but forfeits his soul?"

Many of us think the same principle applies to our nation. What is the profit to America if we have endless economic prosperity, computers and a hundred channels of television in every home, new cars, boats, glamorous vacations, and more . . . if our families are shattered, our children are corrupted; if we forget or throw away the values and traditions that are the soul of America; or worst of all, if we Christians fail to honor Jesus Christ?

Bob Dugan meets such issues head-on with faith, optimism, and a firm intention to reclaim America's heritage of biblical values. He demonstrates how a person can fight for principle in the political world without compromising his testimony.

Firmly rooted in the Bible, the U.S. Constitution and a wealth of practical experience, this book gives believers a solid grounding on major issues, a framework for strategy, and a battle plan for honoring God in the political process.

In this book, Bob Dugan is not seeking merely to entertain or engage your attention. He wants to change your life. He intends to recruit and motivate you to help turn things around for America.

I pray he will be successful in doing so.

Sen. Bill Armstrong
Washington, D.C.

Prologue

At Least I Tried

If decent people do not like
the way politicians behave,
they should either get into politics
or refrain from complaining
about anything politicians do.
—Teddy Roosevelt

July 4, 1976 was the 200th anniversary of America's Declaration of Independence. It was a perfect year to run for Congress. September 14, two months and ten days later, was of no historic significance, except to a few dozen candidates hoping to snare a nomination in Colorado's primary elections. I was among them.

I was hoping to become a member of the U.S. House of Representatives. But first I would have to secure the Republican nomination in Colorado's second congressional district[1] by defeating Ed Scott, the odds-on favorite.

I busied myself in the office, endured a bit of nervousness, and berated the rainy afternoon, complete with hailstorm, which was sure to cut voter turnout.

Several dozen friends accepted our invitation to share the evening with us, to snack, talk, and above all watch the returns on television. Deep down, I suspect, they somehow knew that they would be needed to play the role of comforters, even though our gathering was officially billed as a victory party.

As the ringing phones became more insistent, the moment of truth closed in. Was I ready to make a statement, the *Denver Post* wanted to know? No, not yet. Denver's NBC-TV anchor was on the line wondering why not. Why not? Well, the absentee ballots hadn't even been counted. Maybe they would counter the early evening's trend and turn the race around.

• • • •

I'm surprised I didn't hear it all the time: "What's a nice pastor like you doing in a place like politics?" To many folks, politics is just one thing: dirty. What self-respecting Christian would let himself get involved in politics—much less a pastor?

For one, I would. My chief allegiance in life, settled decades before and frequently reaffirmed, is to Jesus Christ. Two millennia ago, had he not made it clear that his method would be to send his followers into the world, as his Father had sent him? God deliberately, and with infinite forethought, sent his Son from the ultimate cleanliness of heaven into a dirty, polluted, and decadent world. Jesus' birth in a stable—not the beautiful, antiseptic scene pictured on our Christmas cards, but a smelly, dirty barn with manure on the floor—symbolized that.

It seemed to me consistent that God would put his people in the so-called dirty world of politics. Like Jesus, they would enter that world on assignment, to bring truth, justice, righteousness, and even redemption.

And hadn't Jesus himself called Christians "the salt of the earth"?[2] He was not simply suggesting that his followers should flavor society. In the pre-refrigeration days of the first century, salt was used as a preservative. To protect a catch of fish or a fresh kill from spoilage, one should salt it well.

But if Christian "salt" is to fulfill its function, it must be shaken out of the "saltshaker" of the church. To preserve society from moral and spiritual corruption, that salt must be shaken into every aspect of the culture. Especially important are the decision-making structures at all levels—local, county, state, and national. Churches which withdraw from the world or monopolize their people's loyalties and thus deprive them of optional time to serve in the world unwittingly foil their Lord's purpose for the church.

Christian laymen are desperately needed in politics. So are Christian women. That's the message of this book. But pastors? Don't they have a lifetime call to the ministry? How dare they turn their backs on God's calling. And yet there I was, campaigning for political office.

In my case, the "what's a nice pastor like you doing in politics?" question seemed especially severe. As far back as the fourth grade, I went on record as headed for the ministry. On the first day of class, when all the kids revealed their life's ambitions, the boys favored such glamorous futures as baseball players, firemen, or cowboys. Not me. Years later, my fourth grade teacher questioned my dad about whether young Bobby had gone into the ministry. Never, before or since, had she heard an eight-year-old predict with such certainty that he would someday be a minister.

In high school I even took four years of Latin, believing that such a foundation would make Greek come easier in college. It did. That in turn made it possible to take Hebrew my first year in seminary. All along, I knew exactly where I was headed.

That's why resigning the pastorate of my suburban Denver church in early 1975—to run for Congress, of all things—might well have been challenged by somebody with the guts to do it. But nobody did.

My road to the campaign trail began in 1973. A lobbyist friend introduced me to the Senate president, who in turn invited me to serve as Senate chaplain for a week in March and then another in May. One day when a couple of senators and I were playing golf, I suggested a Bible study among the legislators. It would be totally off-the-record, and if no one else were available to lead it, they were looking at a volunteer.

Early that December, Sen. Hugh Fowler invited me to lunch. Unknown to me, he was chairman of the Senate committee which hired the staff. His committee, he said, hoped that I would be willing to become the regular Senate chaplain for 1974. For years they had operated with a visiting-fireman approach, with dozens of ministers, priests, or rabbis visiting the Senate for a day or two or as much as a week. How much better it would be if their chaplain could be there every day, developing friendships and helping meet the needs of the senators and their staffs!

"I would love to," I replied, "provided that I wouldn't be limited to the formal duty of opening the sessions with prayer, as important as that would be."

"That's exactly why we're asking you," he shot back. "When we were playing golf, I became aware how really interested you were in us senators." When Hugh finally introduced me to the staff, he told them, "He's your pastor, whenever you need him." My tenure as chaplain would continue through the 1975 session. Those were great, thoroughly enjoyable days.

There's a political maxim that goes, "If you like baloney and love the law, you should never go see either one made." I found it unreliable. Day by day I watched the law being made, from a seat on the leather bench surrounding the beautiful, almost elegant Senate chamber, with its clear-windowed view to the Rocky Mountains just a few miles west. I was impressed, fascinated. How in this world could law-making be done better than by representative government?

I realized I could fit into this kind of scene—and wanted to. But because my interests were in national rather than state issues, Congress, not the legislature, would be my goal.

I took the leap in January 1975, resigning my five-year pastorate to run for Congress. The last week in February I flew to Washington to reconnoiter. Frankly, I did not even realize I should have gone to the Republican National Committee to inform them of my interest in running. However, one contact led to another, and I secured appointments with Congressmen John Conlan of Arizona, Clarence Brown of Ohio, Guy VanderJagt of Michigan, John Buchanan of Alabama, and others.[3] But the most memorable meeting took place with Sen. Mark Hatfield of Oregon.

His personal secretary emerged from the inner office with an apology and the senator's datebook. What a shame. An emergency required him to return to Oregon that night, and the remaining three days of work and appointments had to be compressed into Wednesday. He really wanted to see me, but it might be impossible.

Maybe, however, if I went to the meeting of the Senate Rules Committee, we would at least bump into each other for a minute. It was twenty-five minutes before I could shoehorn myself into the hearing room. The closest Senate election in history had been dumped into the Senate's lap by the state of New Hampshire, whose Governor's Ballot Committee was unwilling or unable to declare a winner. Republican Louis Wyman originally appeared to win by 355 votes, but the Secretary of State's recount produced a reversal, with Democrat John Durkin ahead by ten votes. Taking another look, New Hampshire officials said that Wyman had won after all, by a total of two ballots.

The Constitution had a provision for this kind of situation. The Senate, the final judge of the qualifications of its members, would have to decide.

Shortly after I found a seat in the committee room, the committee moved to send its chairman, Sen. Howard Cannon, and its ranking minority member, Senator Hatfield, to the basement vault where approximately thirty-five hundred disputed paper ballots were stored, to bring them into the light of committee scrutiny.

As the television lights snapped off, Mark Hatfield

moved from the dais, spotted me, and invited me along for the ride.

Crowding the elevator were the two senators, attorneys for both claimants of the seat, about eight or ten capitol police, and I. After successive vault doors were opened, several unremarkable, used cardboard cartons containing the disputed ballots were loaded onto a rolling cart for the trip upward. I glanced at the ballots as they were spread out on the committee's table. It seemed incredible that so many people could not follow simple directions: to vote with an X, not a check or other symbol; to make sure that the arms of the X crossed within the circle, and nowhere else. Their carelessness or orneriness had muddied up the outcome of an election to the United States Senate.

Senator Hatfield interrupted my reverie. Could we go into a quiet anteroom for a few minutes, so that we could at least talk briefly? Knowing that I wanted to discuss the feasibility of running and to pick up some pointers, Mark nevertheless had some things he wanted to mention first.

"You're going to be in an entirely new arena, unlike the church," he said. "Because some people think clergymen have their feet planted firmly in the air and aren't real human beings, your advisers will want to establish your image. 'Bob,' one may say, 'we know you wouldn't tell any really raunchy jokes to this men's group today, but how about a couple of slightly off-color stories to let 'em know you're one of the boys?' "

For a moment, this senator who takes his Christian commitment seriously turned the tables on me. He was the pastor and I his parishioner. Drawing himself to attention and pointing his finger, Mark spoke forcefully: "Never do that. Never forget who you are as a man of God. It's not worth losing your character to win an election." He then gave me his formula for life's priorities. My first loyalty must always be to the Lord; my second to my family; and only my third to my constituents.

Who wouldn't be pumped up after a week of such

meetings? The members of Congress seemed to say I would be an attractive candidate, that I could win, and that they were eager to have me as a colleague in the House of Representatives. I believed them. And I flew back to Colorado elated, convinced I should run.

How does one get started running for Congress? Obviously, I needed to learn how the political process worked. I needed to meet my party's top leaders and cultivate party contacts. I had to develop a broad set of political convictions. And without question I needed to become widely known in my congressional district.

But first I had to settle a preliminary question. Can anybody get elected to Congress without first holding a lower office? A search through that year's *Almanac of American Politics* showed that about one-third of the members of the House were holding their initial political office. No barrier there.

You can't go far without a campaign manager. Late in '75 we found him, thanks to a mutual friend in the state Senate. Jim Files was a professor at Denver University, but in a position to put a healthy part-time effort into my campaign. He had already successfully managed a Texas congressional campaign for Bob Price. Unfortunately, my name was not as adaptable to a winning slogan as the Texan's "Price is right."

In many states, anybody can get on the ballot by obtaining a petition with a certain number of signatures, but Colorado's nominating system involves a caucus and convention process. Since caucuses meet every other year, I discovered to my chagrin that in my six years of residence I'd passed up all three opportunities to attend a caucus in my precinct.

Several secretly sympathetic party officials brought me up to speed. In my own Jefferson County, they even gave me much-appreciated exposure to party workers by allowing me to train them in special seminars. Over the months, there would be no end of Republican county or state central committee meetings and the like.

Several hundred Republican delegates to June's Second Congressional District Assembly would decide who would have a place on the ballot. The majority would be party veterans who managed to get themselves appointed year after year. I spent countless evenings visiting delegates from the prior year's list. I was impressed with the high caliber of many of those people. They were highly motivated and unselfish, committed to better government, not stereotypical political hacks.

By one means or another, I got acquainted with the top leadership. I tackled rumored rivals for the nomination by inviting them to lunch. I spent time developing my political views. With a conservative political philosophy to systematize my positions, I took to research like a duck to water. There were exams along the way. I spent two tough hours with the Paul Revere Committee, an ultra-conservative group which would brook little variation from its hard-line positions. Another night in a candidate forum, one questioner demanded a simple yes or no answer to eight complex questions—from each of the four candidates. I'll guarantee that he got more than his requested thirty-two one-word responses.

It was a perpetual effort to become known in the community. I had a modest starting point as Senate chaplain and the former pastor of Trinity Baptist Church in suburban Wheat Ridge. Since I was representing the National Association of Evangelicals' relief and development arm, World Relief, on a part-time basis, I spoke in many churches of varied denomination. Of course, I was careful that my message not be political in any way. In that bicentennial year, Rotary, Kiwanis, and Optimist Clubs were more than open to a patriotic speech.

Seemingly endless neighborhood coffees were a great way to meet people and enlist support. The press began to seek interviews. Radio spots were simple to make and television commercials were no problem, given that marvelous device called a teleprompter. And parades. I never knew there were so many in all the communities in the district.[4] We tried not to miss walking in any of them those summer Saturdays, especially when surrounded by our teenage daughter and her friends, wearing our campaign colors and carrying banners. Freshly scrubbed and pretty as could be, they were a great attraction. There was another plus in those parades: the first British double-decker bus imported to Colorado, dedicated to Bob Dugan for Congress, the contribution of a Boulder entrepreneur.

But our basic strategy was to take our campaign to the homes of the people—by walking. There's no way to calculate the thousands of homes I personally reached as a candidate, most often with my wife walking the opposite side of the street. When folks were not home, we left a brochure with a short handwritten note. The campaign ran through the hottest months of the year, yielding an unexpected bonus—we walked ourselves into excellent physical shape.

A serious run for Congress is no lark. It takes extraordinary commitment. For me, the price tallied up to twenty months of my life and about $50,000, some of it in unreimbursed travel and meal expenses, but most of it in income forgone. At today's salaries, the bill might have been triple. A check of income tax returns shows an adjusted gross income for our family of $5,108 in 1975 and $8,513 in 1976. Our modest income was generated only by Lynne's part-time retail sales work and my per diem arrangement with World Relief. Lynne and our children paid a good part of the price of my running.

In fact, one's immediate family are the backers any political candidate needs most. Lynne was totally supportive. When it was over, our son, Bob III, observed that the campaign had strengthened us, bringing our family together in a wonderful way. What can you say about a son who would press into his Dad's hand a political contribution of $350? As his grandfather says, there are times when you feel like you're swallowing golf balls. And what can you say to a daughter like Cheri, who put off going to college because she wanted to help her Dad's campaign?

I was the first to announce, doing so in a press conference at the state capitol on January 5, 1976. That day I learned some useful lessons about the media. One television reporter arrived early and found it entertaining to try to unnerve me. "Why," he demanded, "are you using this large committee room instead of the official press room across the hall?" I explained that we needed the larger room because a hundred of my friends would be coming to witness the announcement. "A press conference is for the press," he bullied, "not for the public. Besides, the lighting's better in that room, and I'm going to have to change my film if you insist we meet in here." As other press arrived, I heard him grumbling, "You'd think he was announcing for President of the United States."

I saw the fruit of his irritation that night on the 10 o'clock news. As the anchorman gave a brief report of my announcement, a picture of me appeared in the upper left corner of the screen. Of thousands of frames of film, channel 7 chose one where I was moistening my lips. I looked like a freak with three lips. But the race was on.

Caucus attendance the first Monday in May broke records that year. The Ford-Reagan contest for the presidential nomination was in full swing, and the crowded caucuses insured that a handful of insiders could not routinely renominate incumbents. Among other things, the caucuses—open to party members living within the precinct—would elect delegates to the congressional district assembly. More than half of the fifty-one who turned out in my precinct favored my candidacy, so I had my first happy taste of political victory.

The rules at the June assembly were simple. To secure a place on the ballot, a candidate must receive at least 20 percent of the delegate votes. The one with the highest percentage would have the ballot's top line for the September 14 primary. Two contestants for the nomination had dropped out before the assembly, leaving just two of us, and the politically experienced Scott took the top line with 65 percent. He seemed crestfallen at failing to keep me off the ballot.

The press tried to balance its coverage of the candidates, essentially giving us three days in the sun: our individual announcements, caucus night, and the nominating assembly. For weeks at a time I wondered if they had forgotten the campaign, though we occasionally got a column inch or two on page thirty-seven of the daily papers.

Toward the end, I thought we had a significant advantage. Our campaign ran a series of thirty second TV commercials on "Good Morning America" and the "Today" show. After Labor Day, we aired four newspaper-advertised, five-minute TV spots in the evening. Ed Scott never used television. Apparently he didn't need to.

• • • •

There would be no turnaround that election night. The early trends became a consistent pattern. Admitting within the room what all our friends now realized, I fielded the media calls and made concession statements. If the television crews wanted to catch me later that night, they would find me at Ed Scott's victory party.

It isn't easy to put a smile on your face, walk into your opponent's celebration, and acknowledge that he has defeated you. Our children didn't have much heart for it, but they came anyway. Cheri remembers how the TV cameras wouldn't leave her face while tears etched a path across her cheeks. Ed was the epitome of graciousness, and he positively beamed when I asked for an Ed Scott button and pinned it to my suit. I promised that we would wholeheartedly back him, and asked my workers to do the same.

The next day the unofficial tally showed Scott with 17,029 votes and Dugan with 7,519. While I could euphemistically say that I had come in second while my opponent was next to last, the truth is that in one mid-September day my dream of going to Washington as a member of Congress vaporized.

Why did I lose the primary? There are several reasons:

• *I was hindered by my shortcomings as a candidate.* That admission must come first. When Jim Files came on board as campaign manager, one of his first observations was, "We need to teach you how to think politically." How right he was. My opponent once remarked that our campaign color, green, was especially appropriate for me as a candidate.

• *I was blind-sided by party regulars.* While I apparently was leading for the nomination, party officials were discussing the matter among themselves and seeking another candidate. They settled on Ed Scott, actively recruiting him. It would irritate me to no end to hear Scott again and again tell how he was not seeking this office, but that his "phone began ringing off the hook with people asking me to run." Hyperbole is part of politics, but a number of important party officials did encourage him to enter the race.

• *I didn't secure the help of enough Christian friends.* One of my big hopes was to bring a host of new players into the political game from the churches. It didn't work out that way. All too often fellow Christians would shake my hand and announce, "Bob, I'm going to do for you the most important thing that one believer can do for another. I'm going to pray for you." Naturally I wanted their prayers, but I came to resent their assurances when I learned that they really meant, "Since I'm doing the most momentous thing, don't expect me to do anything else— not write you a check, not spend volunteer time in your office, not walk the precincts with your literature."

• *I was opposed by a better-known candidate.* The party went for age and experience when it recruited Ed Scott. He had been a member of the city council and mayor of Englewood, Colorado; had served as an Arapahoe County Commissioner; and had been elected to the state senate. Above all, he had been the familiar "Sheriff Scotty" from a popular Denver children's television show, extremely well known to long-time Colorado residents.

- *I was unable to build an adequate organization.* This is the most important factor of all. I was delayed for weeks in filing with the Federal Election Commission. For want of a campaign treasurer, I could not officially file. For want of filing, we could not begin to raise funds. One by one, three Christian friends, each a certified public accountant, took weeks to tell me he couldn't serve. Finally another friend, a non-CPA, accepted the job. Just retired, he and his wife even canceled the second month of a winter vacation in Arizona, unwilling to miss that much of the campaign. What I wouldn't have given for a few dozen more friends like that.

Losing is never fun. But do I regret the time, money, and emotional energy that went into the campaign? Not on your life. Among the millions of Americans who perpetually berate their government, few can say, "At least I tried." I can.

We Americans do not adequately appreciate the political process in our nation. During the campaign, I often recounted a nightmarish 1938 incident from Aleksandr Solzhenitsyn's *The Gulag Archipelago*, by way of contrast:

A district party conference was under way in Moscow Province. It was presided over by a new secretary of the District Party Committee, replacing one recently arrested. At the conclusion of the conference, a tribute to Comrade Stalin was called for. Of course, everyone stood up (just as everyone had leaped to his feet during the conference with every mention of his name). The hall echoed with "stormy applause, rising to an ovation." For three minutes, four minutes, five minutes, the "stormy applause, rising to an ovation," continued. But palms were getting sore and raised arms were already aching. And the older people were panting from exhaustion. It was becoming insufferably silly even to those who adored Stalin. However, who would dare to be the **first** to stop? The secretary of the District Party could have done it. He was standing on the platform, and it was he who had just called for the ovation. But he was a newcomer. He had taken the place of a man who'd been arrested. He was afraid! After all, NKVD men were standing in the hall applauding and watching to see **who** would quit first! And in that obscure, small hall, unknown to the leader, the applause went on—six, seven, eight minutes! They were done for! Their goose was cooked! They couldn't stop now till they collapsed with heart attacks! At the rear of the hall, which was crowded, they could of course cheat a bit, clap less frequently, less vigorously, not so eagerly—but up there with the presidium where everyone could see them?

The director of the local paper factory, an independent and strong-minded man, stood with the presidium. Aware of all the falsity and all the impossibility of the situation, he still kept on applauding! Nine minutes! Ten! In anguish he watched the secretary of the District Party Committee, but the latter dared not stop. Insanity! To the last man! With make-believe enthusiasm on their faces, looking at each other with faint hope, the district leaders were just going to go on and on applauding till they fell where they stood, till they were carried out of the hall on stretchers! And even then those who were left would not falter. . . . Then, after eleven minutes, the director of the paper factory assumed a businesslike expression and sat down in his seat. And, oh, a miracle took place! Where had the universal, uninhibited, indescribable enthusiasm gone? To a man, everyone else stopped dead and sat down. They had been saved! The squirrel had been smart enough to jump off his revolving wheel.

That, however, was how they discovered who the independent people were. And that was how they went about eliminating them. That same night the factory director was arrested. They easily pasted ten years on him on the pretext of something quite different. But after he had signed Form 206, the final document of the interrogation, his interrogator reminded him: "Don't ever be the first to stop applauding!"[5]

Incredible. Why, we Americans could sit in the front row under the unflinching gaze of Secret Service agents while our president addressed us, keeping silent and refusing to applaud, arms folded sternly across our chests. We could write letters critical of the president to the editor of a national news magazine and have them published with our names and home towns identified, yet fear no reprisal. We are free even to organize opposition to a sitting president, actively working to replace him with someone more to our liking.

The more I experience total political freedom as a citizen of the United States, the more I agree with Winston Churchill's incisive comment: "Democracy is the worst form of government—except for all the others that have been tried."

It's true I failed in my bid for a congressional seat, but God turned my political failure into success. To our great surprise, a little over two years later my wife and I would move to the nation's capital. While I would not have a congressional office on Capitol Hill, I would move into an office just three blocks from the White House—assigned to raise the profile and increase the effectiveness of the Office of Public Affairs of the National Association of Evangelicals.[6]

In my early weeks in Washington, two Congressmen in separate conversations told me I would have more influence on the nation through NAE than if I had won a seat in the House. I thought they were trying to console me by saying something kind, but today I agree with their judgment.

The NAE was not well known outside religious circles in the '60s and '70s. Judging by the media, you might have thought the fabric of America's religious life was woven of just three strands: Catholic, Jewish, and Protestant. More often than not, the National Council of Churches was assumed to be the sole voice of protestantism.

Evangelicals were frustrated at being misrepresented, or not represented at all.

Today there's a world of difference. The White House, Congress, and even the Supreme Court realize there are four major strands in our religious fabric: Catholic, Jewish, ecumenical Protestant, and evangelical Protestant.[7] Government and the media know that NAE is the institutional gathering-place for evangelicals from fifty thousand churches in over seventy denominations, and that NAE has become the major alternative to the National Council of Churches in American church life.

Over the years, God has helped us put together a competent team of professionals in Washington.[8] Together we function much like the office of a senator, although our constituency is spread over all fifty states. If senators *respond* to the needs of their people, so do we. If senators *report* to the people of their state, so do we. If senators *represent* their people's interest before the federal government, so do we.

Working with NAE over the past decade has convinced me more than ever of the crucial role evangelicals must play in politics. To show how strongly I feel about that, let me relate the gist of a chapel message I preached in three different Christian colleges.

Speaking about how Christians can know the will of God for their lives, I laid heavy emphasis on human responsibility. Too many Christians sit back and wait for an undefined, mystical "call" from God. Receiving no unmistakable "call," they feel free to follow their own trail to wealth or success. I suggested that students ought to make up their minds once and for all that their life's work would meet at least one of three criteria.[9]

• It should be a *serving* vocation. That word characterized Jesus, who "did not come to be served, but to serve, and to give his life. . . ."[10] Match that up with Peter's reminder that "Christ suffered for you, leaving you an example, that you should follow in his steps," and you have something resembling a mandate.[11]

• It should be an *influential* vocation. How perverse to twist the Bible into insisting that followers of Jesus should aspire only to humble positions in life. God equips some for leadership, and failure to develop his gifts would be tantamount to rejecting his provision. Jesus tells us not to put our light under a bushel basket, but rather to "let your light shine before men, that they may see your good deeds and praise your Father in heaven."[12]

• It should be a *Christian* vocation. It ought to go without saying that only Christians should fill such callings, but it must be said. False teachers in the church are judged harshly.

If it would be admirable to choose a vocation that meets one of these criteria, how much better a job that meets two? And yet how much better three than two? Any student there could have named a vocation meeting all three standards: the ministry.

But I wasn't finished. Could they think of another, very different vocation that met all three criteria?

I doubt the students were prepared for my proposal. Nobody ever had suggested from their chapel pulpit that one of life's worthiest callings is to be a public official, a political office-holder. Yet such a vocation fulfills the three biblical criteria. Serving? Yes, if the politician's heart is right. Influential? Indisputably. But Christian? Listen to this:

> Everyone must submit himself to the governing authorities, for there is no authority except that which God has established. The authorities that exist have been established by God. Consequently, he who rebels against the authority is rebelling against what God has instituted, and those who do so will bring judgment on themselves. For rulers hold no terror for those who do right, but for those who do wrong. Do you want to be free from fear of the one in authority? Then do what is right and he will commend you. For he is God's servant to do you good. But if you do wrong, be afraid, for he does not bear

the sword for nothing. He is God's servant, an agent of wrath to bring punishment on the wrongdoer. Therefore, it is necessary to submit to the authorities, not only because of possible punishment but also because of conscience.

This is also why you pay taxes, for the authorities are God's servants, who give their full time to governing. Give everyone what you owe him: If you owe taxes, pay taxes; if revenue, then revenue; if respect, then respect; if honor, then honor.[13]

Three times in these paragraphs, political officials are called "God's servants." In the King James version of 1611, they are referred to as "God's ministers." No wonder theologian John Calvin called politics one of the noblest callings of God.

You may not think of yourself as a potential office holder, but politics is far more than running for office. Frankly, ninety-nine out of one hundred people who read this book probably will never seriously consider running for office. Nor should they. But Christians can play any number of critical roles in the momentous world of politics—such as putting someone else into office.

Having said that, I must admit that this book is also written for the one in one hundred who definitely should seek political office. Someday, I hope to hear from a member of Congress, a governor, the speaker of a state legislature, or a school board member for whom this book was the starter.

So, I've given myself away. This book has one major goal: to show how you can take an active, God-honoring role in politics.

Is God calling you? It wouldn't surprise me at all.

Notes

1. At that time, the second congressional district was comprised of suburban Jefferson and Boulder Counties, along the front range just west of Denver, with a small section of west central Denver itself.

2. This simple prediction, assignment, or statement of Jesus is found in the first chapter of his Sermon on the Mount, Matthew 5:13.

3. Guy had just been appointed chairman of the National Republican Congressional Committee, a position he still holds. John Buchanan was an ordained Baptist minister serving in Congress. It is ironic that in recent years he has headed Norman Lear's People for the American Way—and been on the opposite side of the culture war.

4. Readers will understand how much I learned in politics, when I give this sage counsel: Never, as a candidate, allow yourself to be placed in a parade behind a unit of horses.

5. Aleksandr Solzhenitsyn, *The Gulag Archipelago* (New York: Harper & Row, 1973), 69f.

6. The NAE was born in St. Louis in April 1942, before the days of easy air travel and in the early months of World War II. A group of 150 evangelical leaders gathered with a deep concern to protect their right to buy radio time for religious broadcasting. With a positive example of trans-denominational cooperation in the New England Fellowship as their model, they developed a seven-point Statement of Faith as the basis of their national fellowship. It has not been changed since ratification.

These founding fathers had the foresight to open a Washington office in September 1943. For its first thirty-five years, NAE's public affairs presence in the nation's capital consisted of a small staff of two or three. The strong leadership and untiring efforts of the office's first director, Clyde W. Taylor, were marked by integrity. Thankfully, long before my arrival NAE had established a good name in Washington. Taylor retired in 1973, and associate Floyd Robertson directed the office until my arrival.

In 1967, Dr. Billy A. Melvin came from Nashville, where he was a Free Will Baptist denominational official, to become NAE's executive director. He is an outstanding administrator and one of the leading authorities on denominational church life in the country. He guides the NAE from its headquarters, The Evangelical Center, in Wheaton, Illinois.

7. Not to mention many other religions which fit none of the four categories, but are part of the pluralistic fabric of our society.

8. Two colleagues have been with us for over a decade—policy analyst Richard Cizik and counsel Forest Montgomery. Richard has achieved a political science degree, a master's in governmental affairs,

and full theological training; he also has run for the state legislature in Washington. Forest served twenty-five years in the federal government following graduation from the Georgetown University Law School. For ten years he was chief of the legal opinion section of the Treasury Department, and for his final five years he was counselor to the general counsel of Treasury. He is a member of the bar of the Supreme Court.

Brian O'Connell has been with NAE since 1984, coordinating NAE's highly praised Peace, Freedom, and Security Studies program. Lawyer Curran Tiffany's career was in the Bell System, where for a dozen years he served in its office of governmental affairs. Special representative Timothy Crater served as pastor of churches in Georgia for sixteen years, and then as administrative assistant to a member of Congress.

9. It was sociologist David O. Moberg's book *Inasmuch: Christian Social Responsibility*, which first suggested these standards to me.

10. Mark 10:45.

11. 1 Peter 2:21.

12. Matthew 5:16.

13. Romans 13:1-7.

Seizing Our Rights

Chapter One

What We "Know" That Isn't So

Although evangelicals achieved a great deal politically in the '80s, they could have accomplished much, much more. One reason they failed to fulfill their potential echoes down from God's eighth century B.C. indictment of Israel: "My people are destroyed from lack of knowledge."[1]

Sometimes Christian ignorance about political matters hurts because "what we 'know' just isn't so." We cling to "myths, as hardy as dandelions."[2] Just as it isn't easy to rid the lawn of those perennial yellow flowers with their miserable broad leaves, demythologizing politics is tough. People know what they know. They are natural skeptics. But if we are to be effective in the political arena, we must peel away our mistaken ideas lest we be handicapped by misinformation.

Myth #1: All politicians are crooks.

Far too many Americans willingly accept Mark Twain's observation that "It could probably be shown by facts that there is no distinctly native American criminal class except Congress." Years ago I would have laughed at the old curmudgeon's cynicism with everyone else. No more. I know too much.

Unfortunately, this kind of widespread skepticism breeds greater distrust and eventually disdain for our system of government. The attitude is poisonous. If the disrespect was generally deserved that would be one thing—but it is not. As with mother-in-law jokes, fairness demands that we stop making political officeholders the object of ridicule.

My earliest forays into the world of politics taught me a lot. I had set out to get acquainted with my party's leaders and its most active workers in order to gain support for my run for Congress. Night after night I would come home and tell Lynne about the really fine people I had met. Frankly, I was surprised. I assumed I would be meeting power hungry political operatives, but instead I kept on encountering genuinely concerned people who wanted to improve their society. With an idealism tempered by realism, they were volunteers in the best sense of the word. High caliber people that they were, most expected nothing but the satisfaction that comes from a job well done.

My guess is that the same is true of the other party's workers. Of course, I don't mean to canonize them all. There are losers in the ranks, including persons with hidden political agendas or selfish ends in mind. The same goes for some elected officials. But as a rule, these were genuinely admirable people.

When I became Colorado's Senate Chaplain I suddenly acquired dozens of political officeholders as acquaintances and, before long, friends. Here too I was surprised at what I found. Don't laugh, because I'm not kidding when I insist that the majority of them were dedicated public servants. The majority—not all.

Take one senator who had become a good friend. One morning I was dumbfounded to read in the papers that his management consultant business had gone belly up. After the invocation, I asked him to sit with me on the Senate floor. Wasn't there anything he could have done to save his business? "Sure, I could have saved it by resigning from the Senate and devoting my full attention to it," he said. Why hadn't he? "Because I consider serving in this body a sacred trust from the people who elected me."

In Colorado, the legislature held a long session every other year running nearly six months. Alternate years should have run three months, but often went four or more. Senators put their personal businesses on the back burner during these months, and I recall several Senate wives confiding how tough it was on their husbands to start over each year after adjournment. Even then, however, they remained on constant call from constituents and were frequently assigned heavy interim committee responsibilities.

In those years, 1974-75, the senators were paid the princely sum of $7,600 per year. I recall another senator taking three unpaid days of leave to argue a case in court. His client won a judgment of $70,000, which netted his law firm a 30 percent commission of $21,000. This lawyer was able to generate in three days almost three times his annual Senate salary. He certainly wasn't in the legislature for the money. Nor were most of the others.

Now, I know there are other benefits and rewards for serving in public life: a sense of power or fulfillment, contacts that lead to opportunities, the chance to run for yet higher offices, increased self-esteem, to mention a few. Admitting all that, I still regard most of these people as genuine public servants. The same goes for a good percentage of the members of Congress, or of your local school board or city council. These bodies probably contain dishonest or decent elected officials in direct proportion to the citizenry at large.

Christians must be especially careful here, lest they violate the Lord's command: "Do not judge, or you too will be judged. For in the same way you judge others, you will be judged. . . ."[3]

Put the shoe on the other foot. Suppose a friend says, "Look, I don't want to hear any more out of you about Christianity. As far as I'm concerned, all religion is a racket and all preachers are Elmer Gantrys." It pains you that your friend has so badly misjudged Christianity. Tragically, she is dead wrong, and you want to scream in protest.

Now imagine how it feels to be an honest officeholder who realizes that you and your friends (suppose it is your whole church!) probably think of him as crooked. You could be wrong, so don't judge.

Myth # 2: You can't legislate morality.

The dogmatism of those who repeat this bromide would be laughable, except that it is no laughing matter. Christians have been beaten into political inactivity by the continual repetition of this line. They have been made to feel that they are out of bounds, somehow in foul territory, when they attempt, for example, to protect unborn human life.

Sincere disciples of this doctrine are very much like a bishop of a century ago, who pronounced from his pulpit and in the periodical he edited that heavier-than-air flight was both impossible and contrary to the will of God. Oh, the irony that Bishop Wright had two sons, Orville and Wilbur! Wright was wrong. Sure of himself, but wrong.

Those who honestly oppose the idea of legislating morality are convinced that any such effort is futile. They contend that if abortion on demand is declared illegal, women will still have abortions—thereby proving that such moral behavior cannot be legislated.

But shall we then cancel laws against stealing because millions will break them? I'm sure most Americans want society's standard to remain firm: stealing is wrong. Whether some citizens make careers of burglarizing homes, stealing cars, or picking pockets is beside the point. The law sets the standard.

Others use this pious "can't" for devious reasons. They resent the pressure for religion-based morality in society, and wish to make pro-lifers feel guilty for forcing their personal moral convictions on others. Of course, they never admit that, if their pro-abortion view prevails, that would be the "moral position" of our society under the law. Then they would be forcing their morality onto society.

Whatever happens, our society will have values. The

only question is, whose will they be? Cardinal John O'Connor of New York put his finger on the problem in his book *His Eminence and Hizzoner*, co-authored with former New York Mayor Ed Koch:

> Public officials, perhaps more than most people, are fond of saying they have no right to impose their moral beliefs on others. That's equivalent to saying their obligation is to make only value-free judgments. That's nonsense. They would have to remain mute about all public policy issues. To make a value-free judgment is to make no judgment at all.

Anyone still convinced that "you can't legislate morality" should turn to the civil rights movement of the '60s. Honest scholars and the media must acknowledge that the civil rights movement was driven by deep religious conviction—just as were the anti-slavery and abolitionist movements in the United States and England. What our nation conclusively legislated was this conviction: "All men [and women] are created equal." We not only legislated morality, we legislated theology.

There's hypocrisy here. Some in the media and academic elite who applauded the moral influence of religion in the civil rights struggle of the '60s are the same people who denounce the moral influence of religion in the abortion battle of the '80s and '90s. In this case, they resist our "morality" because it differs from theirs.

But is not that the nature of the democratic state? All laws are impositions on someone, unless they are unanimously supported. Some Americans were not pleased when women were given the right to vote through ratification of the 19th Amendment in 1920. But the majority imposed its will on the minority, constitutionally enforcing the moral conviction that justice required that women be treated equally and no longer disenfranchised.

Certainly we can legislate morality! Congress and our state legislatures do it every day. Speed limits on interstate highways and social security legislation both flow from tough decisions about the moral responsibility of government. You wouldn't want them to legislate immorality, would you?

*Myth # 3: It is impossible for a Christian to serve in politics
because politics requires compromise.*

My lunch with a prosperous business friend was fruitful. He was about to give me a $500 check for my congressional campaign, but he wasn't going to let go of it easily. There were some things he needed to say. Expressing personal confidence in my integrity, he nevertheless worried that if I became a member of Congress, I would inevitably change—and not for the better. Like all the rest of them, I would doubtless compromise here and there and be the worse for it. He feared that, spiritually, I would never be the same.

I had thought a lot about his concerns before he ever mentioned them. I had firmly determined never to compromise my convictions. On the other hand, it seemed to me that a proper humility required that I be open to compromising my opinions. Who needs a congressman who has all the answers before he goes to Washington? Who needs a congresswoman for whom committee hearings, expert testimony, and thoughtful debate are irrelevant and a waste of time?

Compromise is not a bad word. Husbands and wives who have not learned to compromise have probably long since ceased living together. Shall we vacation at the beach or in the mountains? Shall we go to a basketball game or a concert tonight? Shall we buy *Encyclopedia Britannica* or a large-screen TV? Nobody has it his way all the time.

Likewise in politics. Suppose as a senator I am convinced that $50 million is necessary to help a Third World nation in a time of disaster. Having argued for that amount, I realize that the most the Senate will appropriate and the president will sign is $25 million. Shall I vote against the lesser amount, preferring nothing to a "compromise" of my opinion? But what if my vote becomes the swing vote, and no aid is then authorized? The applicable political adage is: "Half a loaf is better than none." If that's compromise, I have no problem with it. Those who don't hold the high office of dictator must settle for what they can get.

There's another kind of compromise, however, that is unthinkable for a Christian. Should I violate my deep conviction of the value of life made in the image of God to vote pro-choice, if the polls showed that 75 percent of the people in my district favored abortion "rights"? God helping me, I would not make that kind of compromise even to get reelected. Trading a birthright for a mess of pottage is never a good deal.

What I would have done as a member of Congress is purely theoretical because I never made it there. But for four fellow alumni of Wheaton College in Illinois, the situation is quite different.

Indiana's Dan Coats was the first to be elected, in 1980. Then followed Paul Henry of Michigan in 1984, and Dennis Hastert of Illinois two years later. Politically unlike these Republicans is liberal Democrat Jim McDermott of Washington, elected to the House in 1988. House Chaplain Jim Ford says it's unprecedented to have such a delegation in Congress from a school of only 2,000 students—and an evangelical college at that.

This modest congressional chapter of the Wheaton Alumni Club might be a place to ask our third myth. Are Christians in office inevitably forced to compromise? I can hear them answer in unison: "No!"

Myth # 4: There's not a dime's worth of difference between the parties.

It was George Wallace in 1968, trying to justify his independent candidacy for president, who uttered the oft-quoted dictum: "There's not a dime's worth of difference between the parties." Maybe not on the civil rights issue which was all-important to Wallace that year, but the disparities between the parties have always been significant.

Over the years there have been hundreds of billions of dimes' worth of difference between them.

One major difference is the constituencies to which the parties appeal. Republican cultivation of evangelicals has been extended from 1980 through the '84 and '88 elections to this day. In '84, the Democratic Party gave official recognition to a gay and lesbian caucus—hardly a move calculated to attract evangelical support. In 1988, Republicans initiated an invitation to NAE to testify before their national convention platform committee. When no similar invitation came from the Democrats, we initiated contact with them. I was told there would be no equivalent opportunity for NAE to speak to their platform committee.

But there was—someone just didn't want our input. I testified before the Republicans in Kansas City on May 31, and several days later (unknown to us), the Democrat platform committee met in Columbus. The National Abortion Rights Action League received an invitation to provide input, but we did not.

When we first learned that evangelicals would be unable to appear before the Democrats, I inquired about submitting a written testimony. Without enthusiasm, my informant supposed it would be O.K. "How many copies do you need and what is the deadline?" I asked. He thought two copies should do it. Two copies? He should have been fired for failing to make even a pretense of interest in our concerns. Nobody at the Democratic National Committee headquarters was going to remove my staple and duplicate our statement, at their expense, in sufficient quantity for all the members of the platform committee to read.

In 1984, the parties' divergence became especially clear in the traditional major issues of peace and prosperity. Ronald Reagan and the Republicans wanted to make military spending a larger share of the budget, believing that weakness invites aggression. The Democrats wanted to reduce the rate of increase in defense spending and would have ended production of two major weapons systems.

Republicans supported and Democrats opposed the Strategic Defense Initiative, Reagan contending that the Mutual Assured Destruction stand-off lived up to its acronym, MAD, and that Mutual Assured Security through "star wars" was the truly moral course to take.

When it came to prosperity, Reagan's party said people must be given an equal opportunity to compete on the basis of merit, under equal protection of the law. To Mondale's party, economic fairness required unusual treatment of individuals in order to produce greater equality of results. Tax policies and affirmative action illustrated these philosophically conflicting approaches. The rhetoric about a "conservative opportunity society" versus a "liberal welfare state" may have been overblown, but it did help to focus the debate. And in 1988, everybody in America who could read lips knew which party was committed to no new taxes.

To demonstrate other contrasts between the parties, let's move to a range of values issues that became crucial in the election. Positions stated here were lifted from the official party platforms on which George Bush and Michael Dukakis ran for president.

Democrats opposed the federal death penalty and supported gun control; the GOP took the other side on both issues. Republicans supported a human life amendment to protect the unborn and opposed federal funding of abortions; Democrats wanted to guarantee the fundamental right of reproductive choice and insisted on federal funding of abortions. Democrats supported a federally regulated child care system and opposed any religious activity even in church-run centers; the GOP supported a tax-credit approach which would not discriminate against mothers staying at home or religious day care centers, among other things. Both parties supported equal pay for equal work, but Republicans opposed and Democrats supported passage of the Equal Rights Amendment.

When you catch folks arguing that there are only inconsequential differences between the parties, urge them to take another look.

*Myth #5: I'm only one person—one person
wouldn't make any difference.*

The mayor of Charlotte, North Carolina, was addressing the final breakfast meeting of NAE's Federal Seminar
for Christian collegians. Her comments were forceful and
on target. Suddenly she shifted gears: "How many Polish
people . . ." she began. For a split second my mind raced.
She wouldn't be about to tell an ethnic joke, would she?
Of course not; she's not that kind of person, and besides,
she's too intelligent to destroy her career with that kind of
humor. Then I heard her complete the question: "How
many Polish people does it take to turn the world
around?" Pause. "One, if his name is Lech Walesa." Ahhh!

What a beautiful twist. The frequently maligned Polish
people got a magnificent compliment. One of their ship-
yard workers becomes an independent trade union leader
whose courage and humble effectiveness results in his
country's first free election in forty years and the installa-
tion of the first eastern bloc non-communist prime minister in decades. That one man helped change the course of
Eastern European history.

But let's move back to American politics. In the summer of 1983, a teenager by the name of Lisa Bender of
Williamsport, Pennsylvania, struck a giant blow for the
cause of religious liberty in the United States. As a high
school student in Williamsport, Lisa wanted to begin a
prayer club. When officials refused her that right, she took
them to court. With the help of Sam Ericsson and the
Christian Legal Society, she won. Her victory in court
then prompted legislators to draw up and secure passage
of the Equal Access Act.

The lesson is simple. One high school student, faithful
to her convictions, moved Congress to act. In a similar situation, Bridget Mergens of Omaha, Nebraska, ultimately
forced the Supreme Court to vindicate her religious free
speech rights, ruling that public high schools must treat all
non-curriculum related student groups alike. Lisa and
Bridget. Two high school girls. Acting one at a time.

When the proposed Equal Rights Amendment was sent from Congress to the states for ratification, it appeared headed for quick adoption into the Constitution. But that never happened, even though three presidents, Congress, both parties (at that time), the labor movement, and the national media supported the ERA. As one state legislature after another got on the bandwagon, one person who thought through the implications of this far-reaching amendment decided to act. Phyllis Schlafly singlehandedly stopped the ERA on its fast track. This wife and mother of six, an attorney and outstanding debater, would deny that she did it alone, but she was the one to organize tens of thousands of volunteers into the Stop ERA movement.

Here's a name few readers will recognize—today. Wait a few years. Joe Watkins was a young black preacher who volunteered to work in two Indiana campaigns in 1980, Dan Quayle's for the Senate and Dan Coats' for Congress. Both won. Early in '89, Joe became an associate director of the Office of Public Liaison in George Bush's White House. Who can predict what influence Joe will eventually have? But the administration is staffed by people like him, who, one at a time, somewhere got involved in politics.

More than once I've had the privilege of preaching at Calvary Temple in Denver. I particularly recall a Sunday morning in February 1982 when I had tried to build a case for Christian political involvement. When I was done, Pastor Charles Blair rose and said he was ashamed to admit it, but he had never attended a precinct caucus in all his years in Colorado. He promised to do so that year and urged all his people to do likewise.

Now, jump to Denver's McNichols Arena early that summer, where Republicans were meeting for their state convention. I had barely started down the aisle leading to my Jefferson County delegation, when a woman spotted me from below. She charged up the steps toward me, calling, "You're Bob Dugan, aren't you? I heard you speak at Calvary Temple last winter, and when Pastor Blair said he was going to his caucus I made up my mind to attend mine." Breathlessly, she continued. "Now look. I hardly knew what to do there, but I was elected to the county, congressional, and state conventions. So here I am today, with a voice in determining the person we will nominate for governor." She saw herself playing an important role . . . and she was right.

If you were expecting to hear about a one-vote election, I won't disappoint you. In the early 1800s, an Indiana farmer named Henry Shoemaker formed a ballot from a paper bag when his polling place had run out of ballots. He cast his vote for Madison Marsh for state representative; Marsh won by one vote. In those days, state legislatures elected U.S. senators, so Marsh voted for a man named Harrigan to represent Indiana in the Senate. Harrigan won by one vote. In the Senate, Harrigan cast his roll call vote in favor of Texas' bid for statehood. You may be ahead of me by now. Indeed, Texas became a state by a margin of one single vote.

Let's agree to throw out the cliche about one person never making a difference. And don't assume that you could never be an international figure like Lech Walesa. After all, he was once an electrician in the Gdansk shipyards.

Myth #6: Preachers should stay out of politics.

I once bought this platitude hook, line, and sinker. As far as I knew, nobody in my boyhood congregation of one thousand ever ran for political office or helped someone who did—least of all the preacher. Politics occasionally drew a pronouncement from the pulpit, but generally only when resentment or sarcasm was called for. Nothing gleaned in college or seminary days would have inclined me to dirty my hands in politics.

Today, I believe the reverse. If you ever hear that I've written an article for a series on "How My Mind Has Changed," you won't need to be a Quiz Kid to guess my subject.

Take heart! Ordained ministers cannot be deprived of their rights as citizens. Believe it or not, Tennessee had a law prohibiting clergy from running for public office. In 1977, in *McDaniel v. Paty,* the Supreme Court struck down that law, Justice William J. Brennan writing:

> The mere fact that a purpose of the Establishment Clause is to reduce or eliminate religious divisiveness or strife, does not place religious discussion, association, or political participation in a status less preferred than rights of discussion, association, and political participation generally. . . . Government may not inquire into the religious beliefs and motivations of officeholders—it may not remove them from office merely for making public statements regarding religion, nor question whether their legislative actions stem from religious conviction.[4]

I am not urging pastors to resign their churches and run for Congress. Running for school board, a part-time position, might be something else. Pastors ought to be involved in politics in their preaching, praying, and politicking. In the next chapter I will describe what I mean by a "political preacher."

Most ministers and church boards worry that they may jeopardize their church's tax-exempt status if they get into politics. That fear effectively renders the churches politically impotent. The first thing to be done, then, is for pastors to learn exactly what is allowable and what is not. For that purpose, a full legal analysis titled "Political Activity by Clergymen" is included as an appendix to this book.

Two positive words set the tone. First, neither the Internal Revenue Service nor the Federal Election Commission has ever interfered with a church's right to educate its people on moral or political issues. Second, we know of no case where a clergyman has been questioned for endorsing or opposing a candidate, even from the pulpit, as long as it is only his personal view. Whether that may be advisable is another question.

Churches can hold non-partisan voter registration drives or political forums as long as all candidates are invited.

Educational materials about candidates' views on issues, voting records, and the like may be distributed, as long as they comply with IRS rules on neutrality. Candidates may be introduced in a service, or even pray or speak, but not ask for money.[5] Churches may contribute to a legislative, moral, or educational issue campaign, although they may not spend a "substantial" part of their activity in so doing.[6] Churches cannot establish a political action committee (PAC), or contribute funds to a candidate or political party.

As for ministers themselves, they may support candidates or issues while being identified as pastors of their churches. They may lobby as individuals, and they most assuredly may preach about the importance of political involvement or publicly pray about elections. Again, a pastor's personal or public support of any candidate will not endanger his church's tax-exempt status, although he would be well advised not to make a regular practice of doing so.

Should pastors get involved in politics? Of course. If they do not, few of their people are likely to do so, and Christian "salt" will not get poured out of the church's shaker—and society needs that preservative. Salt must come in contact with that which it would preserve.

Myth #7: You can't fight city hall.

Of all the fictions I have listed, this should be the easiest to discredit. For Christians, a one-sentence reminder that "with God all things are possible"[7] should do it.

Beyond that, the simplest way to undermine this falsehood is to point to an instance where city hall was roundly defeated. Look at San Francisco's city hall in early July 1989, where Mayor Art Agnos was poised to sign the Domestic Partners Ordinance passed by the Board of Supervisors. On the day before he would sign, a group of concerned citizens presented petitions with over twenty-seven thousand signatures which temporarily put the ordinance on hold, until the citizens of San Francisco could express themselves in a November ballot referendum.

The ordinance would have permitted unmarried couples to register their partnerships, much like traditional couples filing marriage licenses. That in turn would have resulted in health and life insurance benefits heretofore available only to married couples. The ordinance was regarded by the gay and lesbian community in San Francisco as a landmark for civic acceptance of gays, a model ordinance for other cities. But the petitions caught city hall by surprise.

The results in November's balloting were even more stunning. The temporary roadblock which forced Mayor Agnos to put the cap back on his pen became a permanent barrier. The voters turned down the Domestic Partners Ordinance in the American city with the largest and most politically formidable homosexual bloc. This battle, part of the gay agenda to legitimize homosexuality as an acceptable lifestyle, was over.

The victory came only after a few concerned evangelicals discovered that Roman Catholic leaders were as troubled about the ordinance as they were. As the churches began to pray, they sought national prayer support for their strategic fight. San Francisco churches cooperated in an unprecedented fashion, first to secure petition signatures, then to organize—with professional guidance—to defeat the ordinance. It was a remarkable and gratifying achievement.

Be assured that you can not only fight city hall, but state legislatures and Congress as well. There was a forerunner to the San Francisco confrontation. Art Agnos was involved in that fray as well, as the state assemblyman who in 1984 led the California legislature to adopt gay rights legislation. Evangelicals were not organized adequately to defeat the bill, but afterward they provided strong and compelling moral support which emboldened Governor George Deukmejian to veto it.[8]

When evangelicals fought city hall in San Francisco, they won a victory for traditional moral values, thus strengthening the entire nation. What if they had believed the myth?

Thankfully, they did not. But it brings up a question: How many victories are slipping away each day simply because too many among us "know what isn't so?"

It's time to shelve these myths permanently—for the good of our nation and for the preservation of a heritage worth passing on.

Notes

1. Hosea 4:6.

2. A graphic phrase from that matchless *Los Angeles Times* sports writer, Jim Murray.

3. Matthew 7:1-2.

4. Quotation in Lynn R. Buzzard and Samuel Ericsson, *The Battle for Religious Liberty* (Elgin, Ill.: David C. Cook Publishing Co., 1982), 226.

5. In his "Super Sunday Campaign" in 1988, the Rev. Jesse Jackson solicited contributions from hundreds of churches, in what appeared to be a blatant violation of IRS regulations. Still, the IRS did not interfere. Suppose presidential candidate Pat Robertson had done the same thing?

6. In one court case, an organization devoting 5 percent of its activities to lobbying did not lose its tax-exempt status, while in another case, an organization devoting more than 20 percent of its activities to lobbying was disqualified from 501(c)(3) status.

7. Matthew 19:26; cf. Mark 9:23; Luke 18:27.

8. Sadly, gay rights activists persisted and reversed that result in the 1990 elections, following the first printing of this book.

Chapter Two

What Is Biblical?

Evangelical Christians are committed to the absolute authority and trustworthiness of the Bible. How could they be anything else? Having ascertained how Jesus Christ regards the Scriptures, their minds are convinced and their wills are bound.

Jesus' view is wrapped up in one text: "The Scripture cannot be broken."[1] Each of the three times the devil tempted him in the wilderness, he replied, "It is written . . ."[2] followed by a quotation from the Torah. His meaning was clear: since it is written, the issue is settled. "I tell you the truth, until heaven and earth disappear, not the smallest letter, not the least stroke of a pen, will by any means disappear from the Law until everything is accomplished."[3]

If the Bible commanded, "Thou shalt not engage in politics," evangelicals would not touch politics with a three-meter pole. On the other hand, there is no eleventh commandment which says "Thou shalt vote." I suspect that large numbers of evangelical Christians could not answer confidently if asked what the Bible says about political involvement. If they ventured an opinion, they would probably be unable to cite biblical support for it.

Many persuasive lines of argument can convince Christians that the Bible assigns them political duties. Let me rest my case on an incident recorded in Luke's Gospel:

The teachers of the law and the chief priests looked

for a way to arrest him immediately, because they knew he had spoken this parable against them. But they were afraid of the people.

Keeping a close watch on him, they sent spies, who pretended to be honest. They hoped to catch Jesus in something he said so that they might hand him over to the power and authority of the governor. So the spies questioned him: "Teacher, we know that you speak and teach what is right, and that you do not show partiality but teach the way of God in accordance with the truth. Is it right for us to pay taxes to Caesar or not?"

He saw through their duplicity and said to them, "Show me a denarius. Whose portrait and inscription are on it?"

"Caesar's," they replied.

He said to them, "Then give to Caesar what is Caesar's, and to God what is God's."

They were unable to trap him in what he had said there in public. And astonished by his answer, they became silent.[4]

Without doing violence to the text, I would like to lift two clear principles that are universally applicable.

In the familiar King James phraseology, these axioms are: "Render to Caesar what is Caesar's," and "Render to God what is God's." Since God merits the top line, let me treat our responsibility to him first.

The Bible is its own best interpreter, so let's deduce our first biblical political duty—rendering to God—from the Apostle Paul's first letter to a young pastor named Timothy:

I urge, then, first of all, that requests, prayers, intercession and thanksgiving be made for everyone—for kings and all those in authority, that we may live peaceful and quiet lives in all godliness and holiness. This is good, and pleases God our Savior, who wants all men to be saved and to come to a knowledge of the truth.[5]

Translating "kings" into our political terminology, it is clear that God expects his people to pray for their leaders. In a word, *intelligent intercession for politicians* is our first responsibility—what it takes to "render to God what is God's."

It would be easy to pour guilt over sincere believers by telling them that they are responsible, for example, to pray for the United States Congress. To intercede meaningfully for all 435 representatives and for the one hundred senators would be impossible. Who could remember even half of their names, or know enough about them to intercede effectively? True Christian praying is not merely reciting a string of names.

An analogy might help. Does God expect Christian people to pray for all the pastors in the United States? How about in their state, or in their denomination? Of course not. However, it is certain that God expects his people to intercede for their own pastor and staff. As members of a local church they either called or received their pastor by appointment. And that obligates them to pray.

By the same token, surely the Lord does not expect Christians who live in Colorado to pray regularly for the senators who represent New Mexico, Virginia, or Vermont. But Colorado's two senators are theirs, elected to represent them. And it's a lame alibi for a Coloradan to disclaim that responsibility by pleading that he hasn't voted the last few times. Anybody with a conscience would vote for the better of two candidates, so failure to vote was a failure to support the better candidate. Net effect: helping the poorer candidate by the one vote not cast for his opponent. There was one less vote to overcome.

One way or another, all Colorado citizens of voting age are responsible for two seats in the United States Senate. Those who are Christians are responsible to pray for those senators, letting the people of Minnesota pray for theirs.

Who else should be on the prayer list? A minimum of

seven elected officials represents every citizen in national and state government. It makes a good starting list, one for each day of the week, and can be enlarged easily. Prayer for the president, for example, can be expanded to include his vice president, his cabinet, and his senior advisors. The Supreme Court can be added at any time, as can the mayor and city council and school board in your home town. But I still haven't revealed my basic seven.

I did so in an unorthodox way at the baccalaureate service at Roberts Wesleyan College in late spring 1990. Not wanting to embarrass the faculty and administration seated in the choir loft behind me, I excused them from participating. Then I asked everyone else to stand.

"I am putting you on your honor," I said. "When I mention a political position for which you have a prayer responsibility, silently determine if you know that official's name. If not, please be seated."

I began with the president. Fortunately no one sat down. But embarrassment colored a few cheeks when I moved on to the governor. Casualties continued to mount when I mentioned "one U.S. Senator from your state." Naming "the other senator from your state" brought real downward movement. By the time I asked about "the Congressperson who represents your district," only about 25 percent of the audience remained standing. Had I named the sixth and seventh who should have been on that prayer list—their state senator and state representative—not more than one in twenty would have remained on his or her feet.

It doesn't take a Sherlock Holmes to draw some deductions from this demonstration. If Christian people do not know the names of those whom they elect, it follows that they have not been interceding for them—and that they are disobeying their Lord.

I had one further point to make with the audience that day at Roberts Wesleyan. As I wrapped up my demonstration, I said softly to those still on their feet: "If you have not prayed for each of these at least once since the beginning of this year, please be seated." One man, and one man only, continued to stand.

Who can imagine what God might do in response to the knowledgeable intercession of millions of evangelicals for their elected officials? I mean *intelligent* intercession. If it is not adequate to pray, "Lord, bless everybody in our family, Amen," or "Help all the missionaries supported by our church," then "Bless all the politicians, Amen," is no better.

We need to start reading the newspapers with renewed interest to see how "our" politicians are voting. We will want to hear them speak, perhaps at town meetings where we can meet them and watch them handle tough questions. We may be pleasantly surprised at how close we can get to them, and we'll develop opinions about their personal character and their value systems. Surely we will want to know about their families and even hope to discover whether they share our faith. Paul says that the ultimate end of our prayers is that all would "be saved and come to the knowledge of the truth."

Intercessory prayer for our political officeholders is a clear political responsibility that Christians have overlooked—to the detriment of the nation. But it's also one that can be remedied as soon as you decide to do it.

Intelligent prayer has a byproduct that leads directly to our second duty. As you pray, you may become aware that you are well served by one officeholder, but that another has a dependably disappointing voting record. The Lord seems to be answering some of your prayers, but not others. Since "faith without deeds is dead," after some months or years of praying, you might surprise yourself by joining a political campaign—maybe to keep one legislator or to dump the other. And in this way you keep the Lord's command concerning Caesar.

How we "render to Caesar what is Caesar's" depends on how we identify the contemporary equivalent of Caesar. Caesar was the final, unchallenged authority in the

Roman empire. We can eliminate the president, for his veto can be overridden by the House and Senate. Congress is certainly not Caesar, because the Supreme Court can rule its laws unconstitutional. And the Supreme Court is no Caesar either, for Congress can make exceptions and regulations to its jurisdiction.

Only one "Caesar" remains, and "he" is none of the above. He is the Constitution. This, our final authority, controls even the separated powers granted to the legislative, executive, and judicial branches of our government.

The Constitution quite clearly spells out how we are to render to Caesar what is Caesar's. Article I, Section 2, just four lines into the body of the document, says "The House of Representatives shall be composed of Members chosen every second Year by the People of the several States. . . ." Section 3 was amended in April 1913 so that the people, rather than the legislature, would directly elect their senators, and Article II outlines the people's responsibility for electing the president.

Our Lord expects that the normal pattern of Christian living will find his followers giving to Caesar what Caesar expects. Since there is no other way to put leaders into office in a democratic republic than for the people to choose them, we must be involved. Naturally, we would not wish to offend God by doing so irresponsibly, nor would we want to fail our nation by doing so ignorantly. That is why I add a crucial adjective as I define our second biblical duty as *informed involvement in politics.*

Our Christian political participation will be more effective and less objectionable if it is individual rather than institutional. The church should not try to move politically as a church, but should strive to see that all its members are involved. When that is the pattern, no one can object, not even the *Washington Post* or an Internal Revenue Service attorney.

This kind of mobilization would make a local congregation a force for righteousness in its community and in the nation. What a difference Christians could make if all were politically active at the minimum level, a tithe of its members at the maximum level, and a quarter of its people at a moderate level.

- *One hundred percent active at a minimum level— voting politics.*

It would be hard to argue that anything less than being registered and voting knowledgeably would satisfy the minimum, basic demand of Christian citizenship. The ideal church would publicize registration deadlines, hold non-partisan voter registration drives in the church (possible in most places), and provide transportation to the polls for those who need it on Election Day.

Unfortunately, there's some quirky thinking out there that sometimes gets into the heads of evangelicals. On the Sunday after I lost my election, we were worshiping in a large Denver church. As the first note of the organ postlude sounded, a woman gripped my elbow. "You don't know me, but I know you," she said earnestly. "It's just terrible that you lost on Tuesday. We need men like you in Washington." She complimented me for a minute, making a strong *ex post facto* case for my candidacy. Then, lowering her voice and turning toward Lynne, she confessed, "Of course, I didn't get out and vote for him. But I guess that didn't make any difference after all."

Because I lost by more than one vote, she freely excused herself. But what if the votes of all my supporters who failed to cast a ballot had been added together? Might the outcome have been different?

- *Ten percent active at a maximum level—party politics.*

By maximum political participation, I do not refer to elected officials or to people who earn their living as strategists or party staffers. I mean rather those volunteers who accept the responsibility of working in the party of their choice. Many will serve as precinct committeemen and women, whose ultimate job is to deliver the vote in their precinct on Election Day. Others will be officers in county, state, or local party organizations.

Not a huge amount of time is required of the party's foot soldiers, but a willingness to work beyond the call of duty will lead to recognition and promotion. Inner city kids who've never drunk anything but homogenized milk may not realize it, but the cream always rises to the top. By virtue of their effectiveness, cooperative spirit, and dependability, some members of the party will move toward leadership. A few, who may have discovered an aptitude and liking for politics that they didn't know they had, will eventually become candidates—supported by their fellow party workers.

One great advantage to having 10 percent of the church's members involved in the political parties is that they become a marvelous source of information about candidates and issues for the 90 percent who are doing other things. Their enthusiasm will create sufficient interest to guarantee a high-percentage voter turnout among their brothers and sisters in the church.

• *Twenty-five percent active at a moderate level— campaign politics.*

Not only will the party activists inspire voter interest, but they will also recruit friends from the church to help in campaigns. Each would only need to enlist one and one-half persons on the average to boost his church to the point where 25 percent are walking the precincts with literature on a couple of evenings or Saturday mornings or giving other tangible help. Some will host a neighborhood coffee where their circle of friends can meet a candidate personally. Others will give volunteer hours in the campaign office, help get out a newsletter or fund-raising mailing, or make telephone bank calls. In addition, it would be a tremendous boost if each could contribute even a modest check to the campaign.

If you believe the professionals, these campaign volunteers, recruited by the most dedicated workers, are the people who determine the outcome of the election. Former White House Aide Morton Blackwell, now a trainer of political activists, insists that campaigns are not so much contests between Candidate A and Candidate B, or between Party D and Party R, as they are battles between the activists supporting A and those supporting B.

The Friday before Election Day in 1976, a first-time volunteer showed up at our campaign headquarters, wanting to go door-to-door for me. She confided that for months she had intended to give me a hand, but had procrastinated. She didn't know where to phone to volunteer, and she was apprehensive about whether she would take to walking precincts, or quite possibly hate it. Would she have a bunch of doors slammed in her face? It was time to put her anxieties behind her. "If I don't help you this weekend, it will be too late."

When our group gathered for lunch, she was excited. She had loved the contact with people and felt she was making a difference for me. Indeed she was. Undoubtedly there were hundreds who could have done what she did, including most of my Committee of 300, each of whom could have involved a handful more. Imagine 1,200 folks going door-to-door. I would have won in a walk.

Under any form of government, a Christian's first political assignment is *intelligent intercession for politicians*. Under our form of government, their second political responsibility is *informed involvement in politics*. If our churches resembled the ideal I sketched above, we evangelicals could be a force for the kind of righteousness that "exalts a nation" and against the sin that is "a disgrace to any people."[6]

The beauty of these matched responsibilities is that political success is not left solely to us. When we give it our human best through personal involvement, in an amazing synergy God Almighty, maker of heaven and earth, at the same time works in response to our intercession.

The Scriptures affirm and experience attests that God

works primarily through the body of Christ—the church—
to accomplish his objectives in the world. And even a cur-
sory reading of the Old Testament will reveal how often he
achieved his objectives through kings, lawmakers, or
judges. Who, then, could claim that God has no interest in
presidential elections, congressional legislation, or Supreme
Court decisions in the last decade of the twentieth century?
Spiritually aware followers of Christ ought to be thinking
through questions about how God may want to use the
body of Christ to accomplish his purposes through politics.

Pivotal to the effectiveness of any church is the shepherd—the pastor—who serves under the authority of the
Chief Shepherd, and who must be an example to the
flock.[7] If the spiritual leader does not encourage, (or better) empower, (or best) enable his people to take an active
role in politics, that church may well become almost irrelevant to its community and the nation.

I know that any church that preaches God's truth, even
if it confines its activity within the church's walls, cannot
be totally irrelevant. Spiritually needy people may find
their way in on occasion and be introduced to Christ. But
other churches will have to carry the battle to protect that
church's religious freedom, to provide the best government possible, and to preserve the nation's morality.

Politicians tend to give evangelical pastors more cre-
dence than the pastors give themselves. Politicians correctly
perceive pastors as community leaders with a considerable
sphere of influence. Those who preach to three thousand
on any Sunday may seem more important to them than
those with one hundred in their congregation, but the
smaller church is nothing to be sneezed at.

Any pastor worth his salt reminds himself periodically
that he is answerable to the Lord for the wielding of his
influence. But that's not unique to ministers: "Each of us
will give an account of himself to God."[8] Having been a
pastor myself for eighteen years, I think I can suggest
three functions for which pastors are answerable:

• *A prophetic role as expositor of the Scripture.*

In the Old Testament era, priests spoke to God on the people's behalf, while prophets spoke to the people on God's behalf. In my view, we have too few twentieth century prophets. When pastors do faithfully speak for God, the collective weight of their proclamation can change a nation's thinking.

In his first formal debate with Stephen Douglas, Abraham Lincoln said:

"In this and like communities, public sentiment is everything. With public sentiment, nothing can fail; without it, nothing can succeed. Consequently, he who moulds public sentiment goes deeper than he who enacts statutes or pronounces [judicial] decisions. He makes statutes and decisions possible or impossible to be executed."[9]

To be effective, preachers must be well informed before they can be informative. An informed prophet must read a daily major city newspaper and at least one national news magazine weekly. He makes a fateful mistake if he secures all his news from the electronic media which, by their time constraints, pre-select what he will see or hear. He must have a reliable source for timely information crucial to the evangelical community.

Early in this century, pastors and teachers were respected as the best educated leaders in their communities. In those pre-television days, people thronged to large Sunday evening services to hear words of wisdom relating the Bible to the times. Today we must earn our hearing, for the public is skeptical about religious leaders. Sheer, hard work in the study is a necessity, so that our preaching is credible and compelling.

Informed pastors will do extensive reading so that they understand historic and religious currents. They must become like the "men of Issachar, who understood the times and knew what Israel should do."[10] Furthermore, they need to understand the political process, periodically reread the Constitution, and cut through to the correct meaning of separation of church and state. Pastors should be able to describe the nominating process in their states, with a rough schedule of dates and events, and be able to tell a member of the church how to get started in politics.

Such a high goal isn't out of reach. A case in point is NAE's first president, Harold John Ockenga. His knowledge of history and of current events fleshed out his biblical preaching and invariably made him relevant, so that his Park Street Church pulpit in Boston was respected more than any in New England. How was that possible? Ockenga would explain that preaching was his highest priority, his unique responsibility in the church. Other duties, however important, would have to be assigned to others if they interfered with adequate preparation to preach.

Evangelical preachers who limit their content to a personal, internalized, vertically-oriented message are guilty of shrinking the Bible. God's Word must be related to justice, to conscience, to societal values, to ideological conflicts. Pastoral prayers should reflect awareness and concern about issues and leaders. In the course of evangelizing and expounding the Scriptures, our pastors will be declaring the criteria by which God will judge the world—including the United States. Christians must then determine how those criteria affect their public duty as citizens.

• *A pastoral role as equipper of the believers.*

Evangelical preaching is too often long on what people ought to do and short on explaining how. Pastors convinced that Christians are bound by political responsibilities should naturally want to show them how to fulfill those duties.

Equipping for prayer begins by modeling intercession for the president, the governor, and others—by name, and with some reference to a problem they face. Here's a place to be creative. Once a month, those who wish could skip dinner and come an hour early for prayer meeting, to fast and pray for their government and its leaders. People could be assigned, one per week, to prepare background information on a political leader, "introducing" him or her to a Sunday school class for a period of focused group prayer. A bulletin board with pictures of the congregation's political leaders would serve as a great prayer reminder, balancing the church's missionary map on the other wall.

Why have we allowed our members to feel powerless about politics when they could have been tapping the ultimate source of power through prayer? I don't know.

Larger churches could do it alone, or evangelical churches in the community could cooperate in a Saturday prayer breakfast with their mayor, congressperson, or other official as honored guest. One note of caution: *Do not* allow an evangelistic sermon to be preached to a political audience of one. That would be "using" an otherwise good-faith invitation and unchristianly embarrassing the guest. Evangelism can come later, one-on-one, in conversation between friends. Let the officeholder speak, have questions and answers—never posed angrily or threateningly, but graciously and firmly. Inquire about family, personal and political concerns, and let the prayer time be an affirming and supportive experience for your guest. You will have built a relationship leading to friendship, and your people will know a great deal more about one of their leaders. That will allow them to pray and vote more wisely.

Equipping for participation may involve special candidate forums to which all candidates are invited. Some years back, the evangelical churches on Staten Island, New York, hosted such an event for a dozen or more candidates. More than three hundred people stayed for over two hours, and the candidates were so impressed that they talked about that Saturday night as being the real beginning of the campaign.

The pastor can announce voter registration deadlines and, as mentioned earlier, even hold a non-partisan registration drive in the church. He may be enthused about building the case for Christian political involvement through a sermon, or think it wise to invite a guest speaker for that purpose. Special seminars could teach church members the political ropes, always in a non-partisan way.[11] Aim for the goals outlined above: 100 percent, 10 percent, and 25 percent involvement.

Every church should have a governmental affairs or social concerns committee. Alternatively, a number of churches in a community or state could combine to produce educational materials for their churches, whether issues-analysis or candidate questionnaires. Get some good advice if you do. The wrong approach can create resentment and provoke a backlash that will have the opposite effect from what you intend.

• *A personal role as example of the believers.*

Sermons about political activity by pastors who are politically lethargic will fall on deaf ears. Who would buy a miracle hair-growth restorer from a bald barber? To the extent that preachers or other deeply committed religious people stay out of politics, to that extent our government is less representative than it was designed to be. Like pastor, like people.

If pastors wish to go beyond the bare minimum of voting responsibly, they will need to get active in party politics and in campaign politics. Thinking pastors will set an example by resisting the lure of registering as independents. It is foolish to smugly announce that one is above the fray: "I just vote for the person, not for the party." That may sound good, but it's unconvincing. Independents take themselves straight out of the process by which the candidates are chosen, and thus greatly reduce their influence on the eventual outcome. They simply stand aside and wait, hoping against hope that one party or the other will produce a worthwhile nominee.

Of course, there is no perfect political party. Neither is there a perfect church, a perfect husband, or a perfect pastor. In this imperfect world, choose the party closest to your way of thinking. Volunteer. Go as the Lord did, as a servant. With that kind of attitude, the party will welcome you with open arms—in much the same way that you are thrilled to have a new family come into your church, committed to the Lord, and eager to get to work. How many of those do you send away with "No" for an answer?

Pastors active in a political party will exemplify to their people that that's where the action is. They may also worry about dividing their congregation, but nothing of the kind is necessary. I think of three pastors in particular who became committeemen in my party during my run for Congress. None created problems in his congregation.

One can be politically partisan to the point of actually being active in campaigns, without hurting the spiritual unity of the church. People of both parties must genuinely be encouraged to labor in the political power structures. Neither by clever humor, by innuendo, nor by partisan sermons should a pastor ever imply that his political position is the only option for his congregation. As wrong as it would be to shape a church so that only the rich would be attracted, it would equally be wrong to shape it so that only Republicans would feel comfortable there.

I spoke one Sunday evening in a good church in a community north of New York City along the Hudson River. Afterward, a lovely couple expressed great delight that I had urged Christians to become politically involved. They had heard no such urging in the thirty years they had been members of the church.

They had a personal reason for hoping things would change. Their son, a lawyer and a fine Christian, against great odds had won a seat in the state assembly in Albany. He was reelected with 70 percent of the vote, but now was running for another post at his party's strong urging. They thought he was the only one who could win it. Sadly, nobody in the church would help in his campaign; nor had anybody done so in the prior two campaigns. In fact, his mother reported that when she sought volunteers from among her friends she would often get a disdainful smile and the pious assurance that she need not worry, for "if the Lord wants him there, the Lord will put him there."

"Is that the way your church feels about evangelism and world missions?" I asked. "Do they suggest that if the Lord wants to convert people here or around the world, he'll take care of it? That there's no need to give sacrificially or to send the church's finest youth to the mission field?"

Do you catch the inconsistency? When it came to politics, those Christians thought God sovereignly acted alone to put his nominees into office. But when it came to evangelism, God suddenly appeared powerless without the sacrificial cooperation of the congregation.

Our nation cannot live with that kind of contradictory thinking in the church.

Notes

1. John 10:35.

2. Matthew 4:1-11; Mark 1:12-13; Luke 4:1-13.

3. Matthew 5:18.

4. Luke 20:19-26.

5. 1 Timothy 2:1-4.

6. Proverbs 14:34.

7. See 1 Peter 5:1-4.

8. Romans 14:12.

9. *Political Debates Between Hon. Abraham Lincoln and Hon. Stephen A. Douglas* (Follet, Foster & Co.: Columbus, Ohio, 1800), 82.

10. 1 Chronicles 12:32.

11. There is a desperate need for a video or film series to equip believers with political know-how, suitable for church use. At this point, however, I know of no such series to recommend.

Chapter Three

What Is Constitutional?

Phil Donahue's television show thrives on the contro-versial—the more outlandish, the better. But until the day I found myself a participant on his show in December 1983, I had actually seen little more than occasional glimpses of the program.

Phil's intent for that day was to parlay President Ronald Reagan's November radio and television spots for the Layman's National Bible Week into a national controversy. The president had not simply referred to "the Bible" in his public service announcements, but had urged Americans to read "God's Word." In short, he had dared express publicly his belief about the Bible—his religious convic-tion. To Donahue and much of his audience, such con-tentious commercials were out of order.

The cast of characters fascinated me. Two panelists were to critique the president: a Southern Baptist minister from North Carolina who also served as a vice president of his state's ACLU chapter, and an atheist from New York who found it necessary to tell the world he was a homosexual and proud of it. I was expected to support the president, along with Martin Marty, church history professor, author, and a regular contributor to the *Christian Century*. While Marty did support Reagan's right to make the announce-ments, he obviously wished the president hadn't done so. Marty was generally critical throughout the show. It became three against one, and Phil Donahue wasn't exactly on my side.

One theme kept recurring in the first half of the show: the president had done something worse than malevolent. He had violated the Constitution of the United States. On that accusation, I bided my time. Waiting can create a problem on a show like Donahue's, however, for if you're not aggressive, the hour will pass you by.

Finally, the time seemed right. I interrupted at the three-quarters mark. "Phil, I have a question that needs answering. Several times today I've heard somebody on this panel or in the audience say that the president did something 'unconstitutional' when he made those announcements. It's time somebody explained just how the president transgressed the Constitution he is sworn to uphold. Who will point out the constitutional chapter and verse that he violated?"

Silence. Not wanting the question to get away, I suggested that the only possible text in anybody's mind was the First Amendment, whose first sixteen words I then quoted. But that mentions Congress, not the president. It mentions a law, not the speech, remarks, or media announcements of the Chief Executive. The First Amendment authorizes free exercise of religion, a right the president had used.

"If President Reagan has not disobeyed the First Amendment to the Constitution, then what other section are we talking about?" No one said anything. Martin Marty assuredly knew I was right, and I suspect Donahue did too. But the discussion quickly moved on to other things, without an answer from any direction.

Pity those who, over the years, have "learned" most of what they know about constitutional law from lightweight shows like Donahue's. Our country is plagued with ignorance, especially where the Constitution is concerned.

A Hearst national survey marking the Constitution's 1987 bicentennial found that nearly 50 percent of

Americans thought the Constitution contained Karl Marx's axiom, "From each according to his ability, to each according to his need." Six out of ten thought that the president, acting alone, could appoint or fire a Supreme Court Justice. The same number were unaware that the Bill of Rights is the first ten amendments to the Constitution.

While anyone can benefit from using a hand-held calculator without knowing how it works, constitutional illiteracy is another matter. There is great danger when public opinion would deny rights guaranteed in the Constitution or demand rights that aren't there.

Profound misunderstanding of the Constitution has deeply affected evangelical Christians. Unfortunately, many have privatized their faith, meekly but unnecessarily submitting to the media elite's insistence that religiously-based convictions should have no part in public policy, that we must have what Richard John Neuhaus calls "The Naked Public Square." In some cases, they have even acquiesced in the matter of elections, having been cajoled into thinking that the personal moral qualifications and convictions of candidates are not proper political considerations.

Evangelicals have been rhetorically beaten about the head and shoulders until they are black and blue with one of the most misunderstood phrases of our time: "separation of church and state." Because they assume such separation to be constitutional, they knuckle under. Thus, the question posed by this chapter is critical: what is constitutional?

The "Grand Experiment" that became the United States of America has the Declaration of Independence for its foundation and the Constitution for its political structure. Several years ago Warren Burger, chief justice of the Supreme Court, sent a message to a National Day of Prayer banquet. His nephew Steve, an evangelical leader from Seattle, was his courier. The chief justice had discovered this marvelous quote in the writings of James Madison, and wanted to share it: "We would not have a Constitution, were it not for the intervention of God."

That Constitution—the result of much compromise—was not perfect, but it has served magnificently. Over a century ago, British prime minister William Gladstone (who, from his side of the Atlantic, might have been expected to be critical of our breakaway nation) lauded our national charter: "I have always regarded that Constitution as the most remarkable work known to me in modern times to have been produced by the human intellect, at a single stroke (so to speak), in its application to political affairs."[1]

About two-thirds of the world's constitutions have been adopted or revised since 1970, and only fourteen predate World War II.[2] Ours is the oldest written national constitution still in force in the world today, the source of the United States' remarkable political stability. When Sen. Daniel Patrick Moynihan (D-NY) was ambassador to the United Nations, he discovered that only seven nations going as far back as 1914 had not suffered a change of government through violent revolution.

The Constitution was signed on September 17, 1787, and technically ratified by the ninth state, New Hampshire, on June 21 of the following year. It seemed best to await the action of New York and Virginia, however, since the government could not succeed without them. After they ratified, the Continental Congress put the Constitution into effect on September 13, 1788.

The framers stated their intentions in a magnificent preamble:

We the People of the United States, in Order to form a more perfect Union, establish Justice, insure domestic Tranquility, provide for the common defense, promote the general Welfare, and secure the Blessings of Liberty to ourselves and our Posterity, do ordain and establish this Constitution for the United States of America.

Their foremost purpose was to establish a nation that would be ruled by law, not by men. The Constitution itself is basically a secular document which mentions religion only twice, the first time in the final paragraph of Article VI:

> The Senators and Representatives before mentioned, and the Members of the several State Legislatures, and all executive and judicial Officers, both of the United States and of the several States, shall be bound by Oath or Affirmation, to support this Constitution; but no religious Test shall ever be required as a Qualification to any Office of public Trust under the United States.

The framers made provision for those unwilling to take an oath of office, usually implying formal calling upon God to bear witness to one's sincerity, by allowing office-holders merely to affirm their commitment to support the Constitution. The words following could not be more clear. They have always been observed in the legal and technical sense that no religious belief has ever been listed as a requirement to hold any federal political office.

On the other hand, the voting public may sometimes apply an unwritten religious test. Imagine a school board election in a Bible belt state, with a Southern Baptist running against an avowed atheist. It would be a rainy day in the Sahara before the non-believer would win. Imagine a last-minute revelation that one of two candidates in a congressional race is a "Moonie." No doubt about the outcome there. But one is not limited to hypothesizing about religious tests applied by voters.

In 1928, Alfred E. Smith had no chance for the presidency against Herbert Hoover because of anti-Catholic sentiment. In 1960, the anti-Catholic vote was still a reality, but it did not prevent John F. Kennedy from winning the presidency. A Williamsburg Charter survey in February 1988 found that only 8 percent would today refuse to vote for a Catholic but 13 percent would never vote for "a born again Baptist" for president, and 21 percent were unwilling to vote for a candidate who had been a minister of a church. On the other side, 62 percent were unwilling to vote for an atheist for president.

Given the growing secularism in America, increasing numbers of voters consciously or unconsciously may discriminate against candidates with strong religious beliefs. There are scattered evidences of that in the last decade. In the summer of 1986, Norman Lear's People for the American Way (PAW) ballyhooed an "election project" targeted at religious intolerance in political campaigns. It was obvious that PAW believed there was plenty of it, especially among Christian candidates.

PAW insisted on five standards. Candidates should not claim to be better qualified because of religious affiliation; assert that God endorses their views; question their opponents' religious faith or personal morality on the basis of their political stands; claim that God endorses their aspirations for public office; or accept support that violates these guidelines.

Who could disagree? Frankly, I've not seen many of these "violations" among evangelical candidates. The offensive, overtly Christian candidates PAW was describing were most likely to be found in made-for-television productions.

Do you see the irony here? PAW is oblivious to the beam in its own eye. It regularly set up negative religious tests, labeling committed Christians "ultra-fundamentalists," calling President Reagan "evangelist-in-chief," and ridiculing anyone who believes a philosophy of secular humanism exists. Worse yet, PAW conducted a national media campaign which precluded an evangelical Christian's appointment to the Justice Department, largely on the basis of his personal faith. That's not the American, constitutional way.

The second place religion is mentioned in the Constitution is in a portion added four years later. The chief barrier to ratification had been criticism that the Constitution lacked a Bill of Rights to prevent tyranny by the majority.

While the Constitution was being drafted in Philadelphia, Thomas Jefferson was serving as ambassador to France. That December, on studying the document, he wrote to James Madison:

> I will now tell you what I do not like. First, the omission of a bill of rights, providing clearly, and without the aid of sophism, for freedom of religion, freedom of the press, protection against standing armies, restriction of monopolies. . . .[3]

On July 31, 1788, Jefferson again wrote to Madison from Paris, revealing his intention for such a package:

> I hope . . . a bill of rights will be formed to guard the people against the federal government, as they are already guarded against their State governments in most instances.

It is worth noting that Jefferson's letter did not express concern about protecting the government from religious influence, but precisely the opposite—protecting religion, as practiced by the people, from the government.

It was James Madison's assurances that the first Congress would pass a Bill of Rights that calmed the fears of many. The promise was kept with ten amendments passed by Congress in September 1789, and their ratification completed on December 15, 1791.

America was the first country ever to establish religious freedom as its "first liberty." In the words of the first two clauses of the First Amendment are the guarantees of this precious freedom:

> *Congress shall make no law respecting an establishment of religion, or prohibiting the free exercise thereof;* or abridging the freedom of speech, or of the press; or the right of the people peaceably to assemble, and to petition the Government for a redress of grievances.

• The *no establishment* clause ("Congress shall make no law respecting an establishment of religion . . .") means primarily that the federal government must not give preference to any one religion. No church could be elevated to an exclusive position of favor and power. The clause makes all the sense in the world when we recall how many newcomers to America, like the Pilgrims, were fleeing religious persecution by established churches in Europe.

Still, at the time of the Revolution nine of the thirteen colonies had established churches, six being Anglican and three Congregational. Paradoxically, many who fled religious persecution became intolerant of dissenters in their own states. By 1787, however, four of those churches had been disestablished.[4] The framers clearly intended that there would be no establishment of a national church. Later, by the "doctrine of incorporation," the 14th Amendment would apply the no establishment clause to the several states.

• The *free exercise* clause ("Congress shall make no law . . . prohibiting the free exercise thereof") means that citizens of all faiths or of no faith would have liberty not only to hold their deepest religious beliefs—something that cannot be prevented even in a totalitarian society—but also to express and practice them.

There are limitations, however. While the freedom to believe is absolute, the freedom to act cannot be. If a religion required human sacrifice, society would be obligated to interfere with the free exercise of that religion in order to protect the lives of potential victims.

It surprises many people to discover that the concept of "separation of church and state" is not found in the Constitution in so many words, but I do not make much of that. The word "trinity" is not found in the Bible either, but it is the ideal word to express a historic, orthodox doctrine of Scripture. Not incidentally, the concept of separation of church and state has for years been enunciated in the Soviet constitution.

Evangelicals believe strongly in the separation of church and state, as historically understood. Both institutions originate with God, and each has its proper spheres of responsibility. The obligation to evangelize belongs to the church; the duty to govern belongs to the state. The Bible spells out three functions for the state: to provide order, to promote well-doing, and to punish wrongdoing.[5]

To see how this works out, take the matter of discipline. Should the church interfere with the government's criminal justice system by springing from prison someone presumed to be innocent, or by hanging someone the church feels to have been mistakenly acquitted of murder? Either would be preposterous. Should government interfere with a church's internal discipline by forcing it against its will to hire a certain person, or by overruling its excommunication of an openly sinning member who is having an affair with a prominent leader in the community? Either of those would be preposterous, too.

Tragically, the preposterous sometimes happens.

In 1984, after a week-long trial, a Tulsa jury awarded $390,000 in actual and punitive damages to a woman disfellowshiped by the Collinsville, Oklahoma Church of Christ, for having an affair with a politician. If there were ever a clear violation of the historic concept of separation of church and state, this is it.

What the framers intended church/state separation to mean is quite different from the Supreme Court's interpretation since 1947.[6] In the last few decades much greater emphasis has been placed on the no establishment clause, with free exercise receding into the background. It's as if the High Court has been constitutionally allergic to anything in public life tasting of religion. Decision after decision has seemed designed to sanitize education and legislation of religiously-based values, as if the court's ultimate goal was to achieve a fully secularized state. The judicial branch of government was subtly shifting the United States from separation of church and state to separation of *religion* and state.

In the *Lemon v. Kurtzman* case in 1971, then Chief Justice Burger set forth three tests that would be used to decide establishment cases in the future:

First, the statute must have a secular legislative purpose;

second, its principal or primary effect must be one that neither advances nor inhibits religion; finally, the statute must not foster "an excessive government entanglement with religion."[7]

Current Chief Justice William Rehnquist has severely criticized this judge-made law. Because the three-pronged *Lemon* test is based on a "historically false doctrine," the approach is inadequate for deciding establishment clause cases. And what is the faulty doctrine? Rehnquist asserted in his learned dissent in the *Jaffree* silent prayer case that the court, ever since 1947, has been interpreting the First Amendment's ban on "establishing" religion erroneously. "The 'wall of separation between church and state' is a metaphor based on bad history, a metaphor which has proved useless as a guide to judging," he said. "It should be frankly and explicitly abandoned."[8]

Arguing that "The true meaning of the establishment clause can only be seen in its history," Rehnquist wrote that the clause "did not require government neutrality between religion and irreligion, nor did it prohibit the federal government from providing non-discriminatory aid to religion. There is simply no historical foundation for the proposition that the framers intended to build the 'wall of separation.' " The "wall," he said, in recent opinions has become a "blurred, indistinct, and variable barrier." As NAE's counsel puts it, "The *Lemon* test is a lemon."

Four sitting justices, including the chief justice, are prepared to reconsider the court's establishment clause doctrine. With the confirmation of President Bush's first nominee to the court, Judge David Souter, by all accounts a judicial conservative, we may see a major change in the court's view of that clause. To take one example, such a court would likely declare constitutional an educational system of tuition tax credits or vouchers which would include private and religious education as choices, along with public schools. At the least, the court will move toward greater accommodation of religion instead of continual attempts to produce an absolute separation of church and state.

Absolute separation never has been constitutionally necessary, and always has been impossible in a practical sense.
Given an absolute separation of church and state, the local
fire department would not respond to the alarm—and
should not—if your church building were ablaze. There
would be no need to seek town planning commission permission approval for expanding church facilities. Why not
get maximum square footage by building over the side-
walks to the very street itself? Government, under absolute
separation, would have no right to insist on parking lots,
size limitations, or anything else. If there were absolute
separation of church and state, the crier would not open
daily sessions at a beautiful marble building on Capitol
Hill as he now does:

> Oyez, Oyez, Oyez! All persons having business
> before the Honorable, the Supreme Court of the
> United States, are admonished to draw near and give
> their attention, for the Court is now sitting. God save
> the United States and this Honorable Court.

Given the controversies over religion in public life, the
Williamsburg Charter Project of 1987-88 was a godsend.
It was a blue-ribbon national project designed to celebrate
the genius of the First Amendment's religious liberty provisions and to attempt to construct a new national consensus
on the meaning of that amendment. It was hoped that the
nation would then be able to reaffirm and rededicate itself
to that understanding.

Led by sociologist and author Os Guinness, this project
became an officially recognized program of the
Commission on the Bicentennial of the United States
Constitution. The Williamsburg Charter[9] document itself is
a superb achievement, drafted by a divergent group of
scholars and publicly signed in Williamsburg, Virginia, on
June 25, 1988. The nearly two hundred signers were not
invited as "celebrity" public figures, but as leaders pledging
themselves to uphold and defend the charter's principles.

Judging by the diversity of signers, an incredible new
consensus was achieved. Representing government were

Chief Justices William H. Rehnquist and Warren E.
Burger; former Presidents Jimmy Carter and Gerald Ford;
and the democratic speaker and the minority leader of the
House, Reps. Jim Wright and Robert Michel.
Representing political parties were the chairmen of the
Republican and Democratic National Committees.
Representing the Bicentennial Commission were, among
others, ideological opposites Sen. Edward M. Kennedy
(D-MA) and Mrs. Phyllis Schlafly.

Representing American communities of faith were
Catholic, Jewish, and other religious leaders, along with
the presidents of the National Association of Evangelicals
and the National Council of Churches. Representing education and public policy were the top leaders of the
National Education Association and the conservative
Heritage Foundation. Representing minorities and ethnic
groups were Coretta Scott King, Beverly LaHaye, and
others. There were signers from business, labor, and law.

Most revealing was the diversity of those who signed on
behalf of organizations specifically concerned with religion
and public life. Juxtaposed against evangelical leaders like
Charles W. Colson of Prison Fellowship, James Dobson of
Focus on the Family, and Samuel Ericsson of the Christian
Legal Society were Arie Brouwer of the National Council
of Churches, John Buchanan and Norman Lear of People
for the American Way, and Robert Maddox of Americans
United for Separation of Church and State.

Such a diverse group normally would never have put
their signatures on one document about religion in public
life—unless it were an unparalleled accomplishment. It is.
It articulates a proper balance. While differences of opinion
still exist, these opinion leaders arrived at a new consensus
of principles, the vanguard of a new civility in public
debate.

To echo the famous E.F. Hutton television commercial,
when The Williamsburg Charter speaks, the people listen.
Here are some highlights from the twenty-three page
charter:

The First Amendment Religious Liberty provisions provide the United States' most distinctive answer to one of the world's most pressing questions in the late-twentieth century. They address the problem: How do we live with each other's deepest differences?

. . . the need for . . . today can best be addressed by remembering that the two clauses are essentially one provision for preserving religious liberty. Both parts, no establishment and free exercise, are to be comprehensively understood as being in the service of religious liberty as a positive good. At the heart of the establishment clause is the prohibition of state sponsorship of religion and at the heart of the free exercise clause is the prohibition of state interference with religious liberty.

The result is neither a naked public square where all religion is excluded, nor a sacred public square with any religion established or semi-established. The result, rather, is a civil public square in which citizens of all religious faiths, or none, engage one another in the continuing democratic discourse.[10]

Evangelical Christians, and all people with strong religious convictions, should take heart. Nothing in the Constitution implies that it is improper for religion to have an influence on the government—not Article VI, not the First Amendment, not a derived but unwritten concept of separation of church and state.[11] Only a distorted interpretation of the First Amendment, making of it "an intellectual pretzel" (to use George Will's metaphor), can be used to intimidate religious citizens from becoming political activists.

Once again, the Williamsburg Charter consensus is crystal clear when it refers to the "right to influence":

Too often in recent disputes over religion and public affairs, some have insisted that any evidence of religious influence on public policy represents an establishment of religion and is therefore precluded as an improper "imposition." Such exclusion of religion from public life is historically unwarranted, philosophically inconsistent, and profoundly undemocratic. The Framers' intention is indisputably ignored when public policy debates can appeal to the theses of Adam Smith and Karl Marx, or Charles Darwin and Sigmund Freud, but not to the Western religious tradition in general and the Hebrew and Christian Scriptures in particular. Many of the most dynamic social movements in American history, including that of civil rights, were legitimately inspired and shaped by religious motivation.

Freedom of conscience and the right to influence public policy on the basis of religiously informed ideas are inseparably linked. In short, a key to democratic renewal is the fullest possible participation in the most open possible debate.

The Internal Revenue Code does limit how much of their resources churches and other 501(c)(3) organizations may use in seeking to influence government on issues. Further, the code declares illegal direct participation in political campaigns, either for or against any candidate for public office.[12] It is critical to note that only *institutional* campaign involvement by churches is prohibited; the *individual* involvement of church members is a right guaranteed by the Constitution.

It is possible to argue that these restrictions on political activity by churches are unconstitutional on their face. Oliver Thomas, general counsel of the Baptist Joint Committee on Public Affairs, summarizes the question:

> Once the government has granted an organization exempt status, goes the argument, it may not condition this benefit upon the organization's willingness to surrender its constitutionally protected right to engage in political speech. The Supreme Court has held, however, that the less restrictive limitation on lobbying by exempt organizations (may not engage in

"substantial" amounts of lobbying) is not unconstitutional, at least as applied to the rights of non-religious exempt organizations. In short, it is impossible to predict with certainty whether the restriction on political activity is unconstitutional as applied to churches. For that reason, both the churches and the IRS are skittish about litigating the issue. Apparently, both prefer the present state of ambiguity to risking the possibility of an unfavorable decision by the courts.[13]

Cutting through all the technical analysis, the Constitution gives to all citizens the right to influence their government—and nowhere does it deny those rights to citizens who hold deep religious convictions. Evangelicals have all the room they need to be involved in politics and government.

Those who attempt to browbeat evangelicals into political silence are, at best, intellectually inconsistent. At worst, they are deliberately dishonest.

Let me show you what I mean. When Walter Mondale selected Geraldine Ferraro as his vice presidential running mate in the 1984 presidential campaign, religion became a major issue. Although a Catholic, Ferraro fell back on the old saw about being personally opposed to abortion, but not wanting to impose her religious views on others. When Archbishop (now Cardinal) John O'Connor pressed Ferraro, prominent Catholic politicians like New York governor Mario Cuomo came to her defense, arguing that abortion is a religious issue which should have no place in the campaign.

In a speech at the Notre Dame Law School in September 1984, Rep. Henry Hyde (R-IL) gave an illustration of today's double standard concerning religious input in politics. He read from a letter written to the president of the National Conference of Catholic Bishops which appeared in the New York Diocesan newspaper, *Catholic New York*, on July 7, 1983.

As an American and a Catholic I am proud of you. It

would have been easy to compromise your position so as to offend no one. You chose instead to tend to your duties as shepherds, to teach the moral law as best you can. You can do no more. Our Church has sometimes been accused of not having spoken out when it might have. Now you, our Bishops, show the courage and moral judgment to meet this issue of nuclear holocaust with a collective expression of where the Church in America stands.[14]

Hyde then stated simply: "This letter was signed by the present governor of New York, Mario Cuomo." Touché. Apparently for Cuomo, when it comes to nuclear freezes and the like, religious persuasion is good. But when it comes to abortion, religious influence is bad.

Evangelicals had better not let themselves be bullied by political opponents brandishing separation of church and state arguments. Most of those folks would be cheering them on if their religious convictions put them on the other side of certain issues.

Just as the Apostle Paul exercised his rights as a Roman citizen,[15] we need to understand our constitutional rights—and exercise them. And we must let no mythical "wall" stand in our way.

Notes

1. Mark W. Cannon, "Why Celebrate the Constitution?" *The Constitution*, September 1985, 22.

2. Cannon, 20.

3. Robert L. Cord, *Separation of Church and State: Historical Fact and Current Fiction* (New York: Lambeth Press, 1982), 86.

4. Cord, 4.

5. Robert Dugan, "Preserving the Role of the State," Platform Plank 2, *Eternity*, October 1987, 25.

6. I will deal with the pivotal *Everson v. Board of Education* Supreme Court decision of 1947 in Chapter 7.

7. Cord, 198f.

8. *Congressional Quarterly Weekly Report*, 8 June 1985, 1114.

9. Information about the charter is available through The First Liberty Institute, George Mason University, 4400 University Drive, Fairfax, VA, 22030.

10. First Liberty, 12, 16, 19.

11. I will deal with the source of the phrase "separation of church and state"—a letter from Thomas Jefferson—in Chapter 11.

12. See Chapter 1, "Myth #6," and cf. Appendix I.

13. Oliver S. Thomas, "Views of the Wall," *Report from the Capital*, September 1988, 6.

14. Rep. Henry J. Hyde, "Keeping God in the Closet—Some Thoughts on the Exorcism of Religious Values from Public Life," speech given 24 September 1984, at Notre Dame Law School.

15. Acts 22:25-29; most of chapters 25 and 26; 28:17-20.

Strategizing for Change

Chapter Four

Changing the Politicians' Thinking

"Applause, mingled with boos and hisses, is about all the average voter is willing to contribute to public life."[1] If that statement is anywhere near reality, then evangelicals have a marvelous opportunity—but they must be above average politically.

The Bible and history teach us that there are two ways by which Christians can change a society. When they fulfill their function as *light*, their nation can be transformed through the spiritual processes of evangelizing and equipping. When they fulfill their function as *salt*, their nation can be reformed through the political processes of educating and electing.

During the fundamentalist/modernist controversy of the early twentieth century, fundamentalists became almost totally occupied with their role as light, while theological liberals majored almost exclusively on their responsibility to be salt. With Carl F.H. Henry's pivotal 1947 book *The Uneasy Conscience of Modern Fundamentalism* as a catalyst, evangelicalism's growing involvement in social and political concerns marked a distinction from fundamentalism.

Today, evangelical Christianity realizes that to be fully biblical, it must function as both salt and light. The twin goals of transforming and reforming are as essential as the two wings on an eagle, as necessary as two oars on a

rowboat. The evangelizing/equipping and educating/
electing functions are as indispensable as the two blades on
a pair of scissors.

Hundreds of books have been written to motivate evangelicals to do evangelism and to equip the church's con-
verts to be mature and responsible followers of Jesus
Christ. What follows in this chapter and in the next should
provide down-to-earth assistance to those who want to
reshape society through the political process.

Evangelicals must set out two objectives. Their *short-
range goal* must be to change the politicians' thinking.
That is first done through educating themselves, and then
persuasively educating their elected officials. Their *long-
range goal* must be to change the politicians themselves,
when voting records reveal an unwillingness to change.
The latter involves elections, and is the subject of the following chapter.

For the ideas presented here to work, evangelicals must
commit themselves to a new level of civic awareness. As
mentioned earlier, Hosea lamented the word of the Lord
which warned, "My people are destroyed from lack of
knowledge."[2] Too many Christians are blank slates when it
comes to the crucial issues of religious liberty and national
morality. At the least, they may have adjusted to being
informed only after the fact.

Even then, no one helps to channel their concerns so
that they actually influence lawmakers.

To remedy their political innocence, evangelicals must
become readers. A twice-weekly newspaper cannot be sub-
stituted for a major city daily newspaper, the *Wall Street
Journal*, or even *USA Today*. The last is often criticized as
the "fast food" newspaper, but it includes (albeit with
short articles) broad coverage of the White House and
Congress, stuff that many papers omit. *People* magazine is
no substitute for a newsweekly. Knowledgeable citizens
will read at least one of these magazines: *Time, Newsweek,
U.S. News and World Report,* or *World.*

And books. The conventional wisdom is that 10 percent of the people read 90 percent of the books. Those people are the leaders. That's why I suggest that one component of a successful church youth program should be to encourage the youth to become serious readers. In a 1990 survey, the Educational Testing Service concluded that only 40 percent of young Americans could read well enough to grasp the meaning of a typical newspaper column. If evangelicals are going to influence the nation, their high school generation must become a major segment of that intelligent minority.

On the Madison Building of the Library of Congress, these words of our fourth president are inscribed:

> Knowledge shall forever govern ignorance. And a people who mean to be their own governors must arm themselves with the power which only knowledge gives.

Evangelical zeal, accompanied by knowledge rather than mere emotion, will lead Christians to influence their lawmakers in one or more of these ways: through single-interest groups, through groups with broader agendas, and through personal contact.

Pro-life, anti-pornography, or tax limitation groups are typical single-issue organizations. While they are often exceedingly effective, I offer one caution. Members must not assume that their one issue is the be-all and end-all of political involvement. They must keep their eyes open.

Other groups with a broader range of interests include environmental, teachers, chamber of commerce, farm bureau, and religious organizations—as well as political parties. In local areas, groups may spring up with indeterminate names such as "Citizens for Better Government," whose purpose will need to be researched. It may be some readers of this book should initiate a citizen's group, given a local problem and a group of concerned friends or neighbors.

At a White House briefing for religious leaders from

around the country, Doug Wead, formerly President
Bush's liaison to religious groups, warned that newcomers
who wanted to influence the White House might, by trial
and error, make a limited impact here or there. Instead,
however, he recommended that they consider working
through "the evangelical lobby" already in place in the
capital. Several groups knew the ropes, he said, and could
much more effectively help to channel their input.

Wead then listed just three groups, in this order: The
National Association of Evangelicals, involved by far the
longest and working on the broadest range of issues;
Concerned Women for America, with a membership much
larger than that of the National Organization for Women;
and Focus on the Family's Family Research Council, the very
effective and highly professional "new kid" on the block.

Whenever and however individuals channel their political energies, it will always be crucial for evangelicals to
develop personal contact with those whom they have
elected. There are two reasons for that. First, such contact
is probably the most effective way of persuading, especially
when reinforced by others feeling the same way. Members
of Congress find the positions of most groups predictable,
but letters on one issue from fifty voters in their district
get their attention.

Second, and equally important, the church is clearly off
the hook with respect to charges of improper religious
influence when its individual members are the ones participating in the political process. When churches encourage
individual involvement rather than institutional involvement in politics, nobody can properly criticize them—not
constitutional lawyers, not hostile humanists, not super-
critical media. Furthermore, the church does not become
politicized.

For such an approach to work, all that is necessary is
agreement on the part of the church's leadership and a
decision to provide some reliable, non-partisan, and relevant source of information to the members.[3] Individuals
then respond to items of special interest and the church in

no way controls their input into political decision-making. This is not merely a beautiful theory. It works. When members of Congress receive such grassroots communications, they will not realize an orchestrated campaign is behind it. If they did, they would sharply discount the importance of the mail.

Five common mistakes in contacting government are these: approaching an irrelevant official, at an inappropriate time, with inaccurate information, using an inferior method, with an ill-advised idea.

Irrelevant officials are those who can afford to overlook your opinions because they don't represent you. If you live in Illinois, a member of Congress from California could not care less about your views. Get in touch with the two senators from your state or the one representative from the district where you live. As a voter, you will be deciding whether to retain or reject them in future elections. That's why they must pay attention to your views. There are just a few exceptions to this rule, such as a senator who is running for president, or the Speaker of the House, who must be concerned with his party's overall image.

The most *inappropriate time* is after the fact, subsequent to the final vote. Too soon can also be a problem. Newspapers will give a sense of when members' time is consumed with certain major issues. It might be well to postpone writing about your concern until leadership begins to talk about taking it up, although sometimes voters need to urge, early on, that an item be included in the agenda.

Inaccurate information is most unfortunate. How would you like to be an evangelical Congressman mistakenly charged with voting to support pornography? It happened to a friend. How would you like to be the Federal Communications Commission, receiving over 25 million petitions in response to a phony rumor that atheist Madalyn Murray O'Hair is trying to remove all religious broadcasting from the air? That also happened, starting in the '70s, and it hasn't stopped yet.

Inferior methods of communication include group letters and/or petitions, pre-printed postcards, and form letters. They are perceived as resulting from organized efforts and have less impact. I can imagine one person at her kitchen table, with different colored pens and imaginative writing styles, signing twenty-five different names. One personally written letter is equivalent to the whole stack.

Ill-advised ideas are easy to envision. One angry constituent wrote a senator to ask that daylight savings time be rescinded, because the extra hour of sunlight was scorching his lawn. Some apparently serious ideas may sound good—until thought through. A bill to outlaw the portrayal of violence on television, once actually proposed, seemed worthy enough until it was pointed out that such a law would not only prohibit the showing of gratuitous violence, but also World War II newsreel footage or a dramatization of the crucifixion of Christ.

Those who wish to be effective in writing to the members of Congress, the president, their governor, their state legislators, and others, will follow several tested guidelines:

• *Be correct.* Errors of name, etiquette, or spelling will diminish the impact of any letter. The proper forms for letters to Congress or the president are found in a footnote at the end of this chapter.[4]

• *Be courteous.* An honest element of appreciation at the beginning sets an excellent tone. Never threaten. Avoid harshness, anger, sarcasm, or a condescending tone. Don't become a nuisance as a regular "pen pal."

• *Be clear.* If letterhead is not used, provide a return address and a legible signature. Business or professional letterhead may impress, although care must be taken so that a businessman from New York City, for example, makes clear that he has written to a congressman from Connecticut because he resides there. Refer to a specific bill by name and number. State clearly what you want, whether asking him to cosponsor a bill, request a hearing, or vote a certain way.

• *Be concise.* A letter should deal with only one subject because it will be directed to a legislative assistant specializing in that issue. A second or third subject might be lost in office routing. An ideal letter will be one page long.

• *Be convincing.* Using your own words (staff will spot identical typed or handwritten copies of a "sample" letter suggested in a church bulletin), express yourself persuasively on why you feel strongly for or against your subject. In the process, you might even give a senator an argument she can use to win over colleagues or constituents.

• *Be constructive.* A writer who suggests how a bill could be amended to make it acceptable provides a great service to an officeholder. Ask for a reply, to be sure that your letter gets proper attention. If a congressman votes according to your wishes, a thank you note is always appropriate.

Telephone calls to your senators or representative need not be long distance. Senators will have several offices in their state, and a congressman will have one or more depending on the size of his district. The phone is especially useful when time is of the essence—for example, when there is a vote the next day. Calls will be tabulated and reported, but letters allow explanations rather than just yea or nay opinions. Generally, calls from strangers are not overly productive, so that the phone is a better tool when a member or staffer knows the caller.

Visits with members of Congress are sometimes possible in their Washington offices, by advance appointment. Many of the suggestions above concerning letter writing should be adapted for a visit, e.g., instead of one page, you may be limited to ten minutes. Visits in your state or district are much more likely. Almost any citizen who wants to do so can meet his senators and representatives within the next six months. Read their mailings about town meetings or watch the papers for where they will speak. Go. Ask questions. Form a personal impression of them. You can become part of the small percentage of Americans who actually change the thinking of their elected officials.

For the sake of completeness, let me add that minds can also be changed by persuasive letters to the editor and guest columns in local papers and by wisdom which makes itself heard amid the banal chit-chat of radio talk shows.

Some of you may be thinking, *but do contacts with members of Congress make any difference?* The answer is Yes, according to 219 top congressional staff members surveyed by the *Washingtonian* magazine in 1983. The factors most influencing the decisions of the lawmakers were, in order of priority: 1) a member's political philosophy; 2) constituent opinion; 3) office mail; 4) the White House; 5) party leaders; 6) the press back home; 7) Washington lobbies; and 8) the national media.[5]

In May 1983, I testified before a Senate committee concerning President Reagan's constitutional amendment regarding prayer in schools. In an unusual move, Sen. Orrin Hatch (R-UT) called me back to the microphone later that afternoon. He wanted to clarify the position of other parts of the religious community. He concluded by asking me to plead with Christians to write him and their senators, who "need to know" public sentiment on the matter of school prayer.

My evangelical brothers and sisters occasionally cause heartburn—sometimes by their use of the Bible in the political arena, and other times by their attitudes in exerting pressure. Too often I have watched a Christian wave his Bible in the air at a committee hearing, and embarrassingly call for a legislative body to enforce it. Where the Bible is concerned, the wisdom of attorney-theologian John Warwick Montgomery commends itself:

> Believers should strive to legislate all those socially valuable moral teachings of Scripture whose value can be meaningfully argued for in a pluralistic society. In such areas (e.g., right-to-life, equal pay for equal work, etc.) evangelicals must not engage in "Christian crusades," implying that it's "Christians vs. pagans," but should offer arguments on scientific, social, and ethical grounds potentially meaningful to

the non-Christian. Even if unbelievers are not convinced, they can see that Christians are making their case on grounds which they themselves must confess to be legitimate in a pluralistic society. Then, even though believers vote en bloc and pass the legislation, the non-Christian has no right to claim that an alien religion is being imposed on him.[6]

Evangelicals must not lose their distinct Christian witness as they operate in the political realm. Former Ohio State football coach Woody Hayes, an advocate of four-yards-and-a-cloud-of-dust ground control football, used to defend his style of play by observing, "When you put a football into the air three things can happen, and two of them aren't good."

Well, when you put evangelicals into the political game, three things can happen, and two of them aren't good either. Those evangelicals can lose, or they can win, or they can win the battle while losing their testimony. In the 1984 struggle over a Christian school in Nebraska, many so-called Christians hassled state legislators with repeated telephone calls from midnight to the wee hours of the morning. That same year, far too many other alleged Christians phoned Capitol Hill with the message that their senator was going to hell if he didn't vote for equal access. Not only was that message unkind, it's unbiblical. It would be better for such persons to stay away from politics than to cast a shadow on the name of Christ.

Unfortunately, I have watched too many Christians in politics display anger, animosity, and even outright hatred toward their political "enemies." How could they be unaware of Jesus' command to "Love your enemies"? Did they with malice aforethought ignore it? Or could they think he excluded political foes from his command?

Not only is it right to treat all political leaders Christianly, but, pragmatically, it works in the long run. Bitterness is counter-productive in dealing with elected officials, from the president down to city council or school board members.

I think of one memorable illustration of this in Madalyn Murray O'Hair, the aggressive atheist who played a significant role in removing devotional Bible reading from America's schools in 1963. One day I received a last-minute request from Cable News Network to appear on a national call-in show to debate Mrs. O'Hair about prayer in schools. By "coincidence" I met Bill Murray, O'Hair's son, at the airport. At that time he had come far enough to believe in God; later he would clearly become a Christian.

When I arrived at the CNN studios I was introduced to Mrs. O'Hair. She treated me like dirt. As we moved onto the set, she sneered, "I'm going to destroy you out here."

Waiting for the show to start, I prayed silently. My only request was that God would help me to be Christ-like in my responses. I felt sure that after the program viewers would recall my attitudes more than my arguments. What I hadn't considered was that they would remember O'Hair's attitudes more than her arguments, too.

The moderator, Sandy, allowed Madalyn to begin. She warmed up by referring to me as a member of the National Association of Religious Nuts. I listened as she flailed wildly at me and took coarse verbal swings at Christians everywhere. When my turn came, she butted in before I completed a single sentence and kept it up throughout the program. The names she used on the air were worse than anything I've ever been called, but she really vented her spleen when we went off the air for a commercial.

Viewers took note. The first bunch of callers directed considerable sympathy toward me. During the half-time break, I asked Sandy for the lead when we returned, since Madalyn had dominated the first half.

"Sandy," I said when we began again, "I am in the unusual position of being able to bring personal greetings to Mrs. O'Hair from her son Bill, whom I met a little over three hours ago at Washington's National Airport. Our viewers might be fascinated to know why Bill Murray came to the capital tonight. Tomorrow afternoon he hopes to testify before a House Judiciary subcommittee about prayer in schools. He wants to help undo the terrible wrong done when he was used by his mother, as a boy of fourteen, in a suit to remove prayer and Bible reading from schools."

Madalyn was apoplectic. "He knows where the money is," she sputtered. "He's on the religious gravy train and he'll be tithing the proceeds to the atheists." The studio audience seemed unconvinced.

Before it was over, Sandy got on her high horse and berated O'Hair for several minutes, accusing her of attacking me undeservedly, lacking the manners to give me the courtesy I had shown her, and committing several other misdemeanors. It was hard to keep a smile off my face.

Leaving the studio, I offered my hand and a polite, "Good night, Mrs. O'Hair." Turning on her heel, she spat, "It was not." Viewers saw that night the difference between the fruit of atheism and the fruit of the Spirit.[7] I make no reference whatever to physical appearance when I say that Madalyn Murray O'Hair is the ugliest person I have ever met. It drives her crazy when Christians suggest it, but we should pray for her.

What do evangelicals want?

Over the years, I have sometimes spoken on the subject, "What do evangelicals really want in politics?" Listeners are sometimes disarmed on discovering that evangelicals are not guilty of the recurring charge that they have no political agenda beyond a couple of personal morality issues. On a broad range of issues, evangelicals have been and will continue to influence politicians' thinking.

On our agenda are six social values principles. Rooted as they are in biblical truth, most evangelicals will unashamedly subscribe to them. Still, it is important to acknowledge that sincere believers may differ on how these principles may be realized, when it comes to specific policy prescriptions.

For example, let's assume that nearly all evangelicals concur that lifting the United States' national debt to a ceiling approaching $3.5 trillion is a moral evil, and that biblical justice requires government to live more responsibly and within its means. Failure to take steps to bring federal budgets into balance is thus irresponsible, unfairly burdening the next generations of Americans to pay interest on this generation's overspending. But by what policy prescription shall we begin to discipline ourselves? Shall we take the medicine of higher taxes? Of significantly reduced spending? Or of a combination of increased revenues and spending cuts? Evangelicals will be found holding and vigorously defending each of these options.

Preeminence of Religious Liberty

Religious liberty is the first liberty in the Bill of Rights. That is fitting and proper for a God-given right, and so it is at the top of an evangelical agenda. If religious liberty can be restricted, reduced, or rescinded, then our basic right to protest government action is diminished.

"Proclaim liberty throughout the land,"[8] is inscribed on the historic Liberty Bell in Philadelphia's Constitution Hall. For Christians, the ultimate importance of such freedom lies in Jesus' words, "Then you will know the truth, and the truth will set you free."[9] Without religious liberty, men and women can be deprived of the eternally important opportunity to consider the claims of Jesus Christ.

Government must not infringe upon religious freedom by entangling itself in the affairs of America's churches, synagogues, and religious schools. When I first came to Washington, evangelicals were troubled about the threat of H.R. 41. Introduced in the prior Congress out of concern for financial abuses among religious groups, it would have required churches and Christian organizations to report their contributors to the government. Fortunately, no such proposal is a threat today. The bill was shelved, partly because the Evangelical Council for Financial Accountability was developed to allow evangelicals to police themselves. No other segment of the religious community has a like organization.

Thomas Jefferson said it best: "Eternal vigilance is the price of liberty." Thus, evangelicals must sometimes even join in friend-of-the-court briefs, re: unpopular religious groups, or form broad and otherwise unlikely coalitions to defend religious liberty. In the summer of 1990, we did not hesitate to build a coalition including such divergent groups as the ACLU, Christian Legal Society, People for the American Way, and NAE, to develop and support the Religious Freedom Restoration Act, designed to overcome a drastic decision of the Supreme Court. In *Oregon v. Smith*, the court all but nullified the Free Exercise clause of the First Amendment as a defense for religious groups. Religious liberty had been jeopardized.

Profession of Public Faith in God

On April 30, 1789, George Washington placed his hand on an open Bible on the balcony of Federal Hall in New York City and repeated the oath of office prescribed in the Constitution.

Then, after pausing briefly, Washington electrified the hushed crowd by adding his own words: "I swear, so help me God." A murmur spread through the crowd and the inaugural party. This was not part of the oath of office, although the precedent set by Washington has been followed by every president since. Then Washington bent over and kissed the Bible. Another murmur. Judge Livingston turned to the thousands below and cried out: "Long live George Washington, President of the United States!" The people cheered, church bells rang, and cannons fired.[10]

Simply put, America historically has acknowledged God's existence and his sovereignty. Evangelicals are grateful for that, believing that "Blessed is the nation whose God is the Lord."[11] In the dark days of the Civil War, President Lincoln designated a day in April 1863 as a national day of prayer. Here is the opening statement of his proclamation:

Whereas the Senate of the United States, devoutly recognizing the Supreme Authority and just government of Almighty God in all the affairs of men and nations, has, by a resolution, requested the President to designate and set apart a day for national prayer and humiliation; and whereas it is the duty of nations, as well as of men, to own their dependence upon the overruling power of God, to confess their sins and transgressions in humble sorrow, yet with assured hope, that genuine repentance will lead to mercy and pardon, and to recognize the sublime truth announced in the Holy Scriptures, and proven by all history, that those nations only are blessed whose God is the Lord.[12]

On July 11, 1955, Congress passed a bill to place the inscription "In God We Trust" on all currency and coins. On July 3 the following year, President Eisenhower signed into law a bill making "In God We Trust" the United States' national motto.

Evangelicals believe that national recognition of "the God who is there," to use Francis Schaeffer's memorable phrase, is essential for the blessing of the Lord of history. That acknowledgment is symbolized in the military chaplaincy, national days of prayer, and such a specific resolution as Congress' declaring 1983 to be "The Year of the Bible."

Protection of Life as Sacred

Statistically, the most dangerous place to be in America is in a mother's womb. Abortion, not many years ago regarded as contradictory to a doctor's commitment to save life, is the most commonly performed surgical procedure today. Evangelicals are more nearly unanimous in opposing this surpassing moral evil of abortion on demand than on any other, and rightly so.

Human beings are the culmination of creation, made "in the image of God,"[13] and thus able to enjoy fellowship with God. Note that "There are six things the Lord hates, seven that are detestable to him," among which are "hands that shed innocent blood."[14] The fact that evangelical conviction on this practice is religiously based does not matter. In American politics, the source of an idea makes no difference whatever. It may arise from religion, a brainstorm, or a television docudrama. The legitimacy of the idea is established through reasoned debate and rests on its content.

Many politicians voting "pro-choice" claim they are "personally opposed" to abortion. But how can one find a practice immoral and not be publicly opposed to it? Would anyone respect a late twentieth century argument that "I'm personally opposed to slavery, but I feel I should not force my views on others"? To the contention that "a woman has the right to control her own body," we answer, "Once you are pregnant, we're talking about two bodies." Americans love the freedom to choose, so pro-abortionists hammer on the theme of a woman's right of choice. Fine, but nobody I know boasts of being pro-choice on racial discrimination. Then why is it considered legitimate to take the life of a yet-to-be-born child?

Americans are living with contradiction about abortion. In one poll, 60 percent said that a woman should have the right to choose an abortion, while 70 percent said the unborn should be protected. Thirty-seven percent answered yes to both questions. The fact is that the majority of Americans oppose the majority of abortions—those done because birth control failed (about half), because a potential birth would be inconvenient, or for sex selection.

The sanctity of life is not just a birth issue. Evangelicals will never accept euthanasia (so-called "mercy killing"), but there will be legitimate debate about artificially extending the process of dying and about a clear definition of when death occurs. The nation must reverse the situation where decisions are made with an ambiguous "quality of life" standard, rather than "sanctity of life" as a clear and compelling one.

It took decades for this nation to conclude that slavery was evil. However long it takes to convince the United

States that abortion is evil, evangelicals will stay in the battle.

Provision of Justice for All

Evangelicals wholeheartedly conclude their pledge of allegiance to the flag with ". . . and justice for all." That reflects perfectly the character of the Creator, who reveals himself as a just God and who has said, "Let justice roll on like a river, righteousness like a never-failing stream!"[15] Charles Colson points out that the biblical word "justice" is misunderstood if we think only of its secular definition: getting one's due. Rather, the word means "righteousness," as in the parallel clauses in Amos. He writes that our call to justice is "to bring the Lord's righteousness to individuals and the structures of society."[16]

Justice to the poor? One of the tragedies of American life is the development of a potentially permanent underclass in our large cities—poorly educated, attracted to crime, and living at public expense. Aid to Families with Dependent Children welfare, tragically, spurs the breakdown of the family, discourages marriage, and rewards out-of-wedlock childbearing. Babies keep having babies. It is not easy to change such policies, but it must be done. The poor must be empowered to escape dependence, but as George Barnard Shaw once said, "A government which robs Peter to pay Paul can always depend on the support of Paul."

Reaction to injustice can produce an equally unacceptable reverse injustice, as in a case involving the Virginia Employment Commission. It rigged civil service test percentiles entirely on the basis of race, to give certain racial minorities a huge advantage over other test-takers.[17] What ever happened to justice for all?

In 1988, one of every four American children was living with one parent. About $18.6 billion in child support payments should have changed hands, but only $4.6 billion was paid.[18] Justice demands that absentee fathers keep their commitments.

Justice demands many things: That the criminal justice

system be reformed to reflect biblical values;[19] that the guilty not so often be free while the innocent are terrified; that victims not be ignored when justice is served; that AIDS not be made a politically protected disease; that parents, through tax credits or vouchers, be able to educate their children in the school of their choice, whether public or private, rather than being economically forced to send them to a government monopoly school which undercuts their values; that taxes be increased significantly on alcoholic beverages and cigarettes, since their use costs society far more than even the highest current revenue proposals would return; and that our young be protected from child abuse. There is no end to such a list of concerns, if all are to receive justice.

Preservation of the Traditional Family

Evangelicals must not capitulate to the sinister agenda of social engineers who, given vaguely written legislation, would assume functions that families should fulfill—indeed, functions assigned to the family by God. Above all, government policies must not usurp parental authority and responsibility for the decisions of minor children as, for example, in allowing abortion without parental consent. The biblical assignment is clear: "If anyone does not provide for his relatives, and especially for his immediate family, he has denied the faith and is worse than an unbeliever."[20]

Historically, the family has been the cornerstone of American society. This fundamental building block has been composed of a married man and woman who have transmitted moral values to their children—not any conglomeration sharing a kitchen for more than three months. Promiscuity was recognized as a threat to family life, and evangelicals and millions of others regard it so to this day. Thus, there is a terrible sense of foreboding as pornography has become a widespread plague, and as homosexuals blatantly flaunt their lifestyles and seek to have their relationships and practices legitimized by government.

Shifting tax policies have penalized families severely. In 1960, 59.9 percent of federal revenues came from individuals and families, with corporations providing 23.2 percent. By 1985, the business share had shrunk to 8.5 percent, while revenue from families and individuals had ballooned to 80.7 percent. To put it another way, in 1948 the average family of four paid just 2 percent of its total income in federal taxes; by the late '80s, that same family was turning over 24 percent of its income to the federal government.

Child care legislation advanced by Congress in the 101st Congress was seriously flawed because it discriminated against a full range of parental choice, whether against religious day care services or against families where one parent forgoes income from the marketplace to rear children at home.

A large bundle of policies will be found under the umbrella of "pro-family" issues. Evangelicals will be found fighting for those policies for years to come.

Promotion of Judeo-Christian Values in Education and Legislation

Columnist William Raspberry put his finger on the problem:

Almost too late, there seems to be developing a consensus that we'd better get busy teaching our children moral values . . . *somebody* ought to be teaching our children right from wrong—building their character.[21]

The *Wall Street Journal* reported that, in a 1990 survey, 84 percent of public school parents want moral values taught in school, while most teachers shy away from that assignment. Educational horror stories like the following seem incredible. A high schooler returning a lost bank bag with thousands of dollars in it is mocked by classmates as a fool. After discussion, his teacher refuses to say whether the honest student did the right thing or not, rationalizing, "I have no right to push my moral values on the students." But education cannot be value-neutral. In this instance, neutrality supports immorality by refusing to condemn dishonesty.

We are losing our moral consensus as a nation, and that will ultimately cause the Republic to crumble. The Bible states: "Where there is no revelation, the people cast off restraint."[22] I have seen no more accurate description of American society today. Fewer and fewer possess knowledge of biblical teaching or embrace its individual and national standards.

Is it likely that we can restore Judeo-Christian values to education? Long-time congressman and then governor of Minnesota Al Quie once told me of his frustration on this score. His blue-ribbon governor's committee was assigned the task of devising a way to teach values in Minnesota's public school system. The committee sought to draw up a list of commonly accepted values that could be taught without reference to religion. When Quie suggested the word "fidelity" for the list, his own committee turned their governor down. Why? The word "sounded too religious." Imagine rejecting a strong value like fidelity, a word pertinent to keeping contracts or marriage vows! The incident symbolizes the titanic struggle over values in our society.

Right and wrong are being stood on their heads. Homosexuality is celebrated as virtuous because it is a radical expression of human freedom. The ACLU battles to prohibit chastity's being recommended in a sex education curriculum because it is a religious teaching. Members of Congress only slap the wrist of a fellow member guilty of flagrant immorality and illegal actions, and voters continue to return to office a representative who was censured for seducing an under-age House page.

America's traditional values are essential to make democracy and a free economy succeed. Yet, those values are often hard to come by in Congress, the White House, governors' mansions, and state legislatures. Evangelicals have their short-range assignment cut out for them—to change their politicians' thinking.

Notes

1. Richard Cizik, ed., *The High Cost of Indifference* (Ventura, California: Regal Books, 1984), 94.

2. Hosea 4:6.

3. The National Association of Evangelicals has for more than a dozen years published a four-page monthly newsletter, *NAE Washington Insight*. In recent years, a shorter, bulletin insert-sized church edition of *Insight* has been available for bulk distribution through church bulletins or mailings. Write NAE Office of Public Affairs, 1023 15th Street NW, Suite 500, Washington, DC 20005 for information.

4. To write the president: The President, The White House, Washington, DC 20500, Dear Mr. President. To write a senator: The Hon. (Name), United States Senate, Washington, DC 20510, Dear Senator (Name). To write a congressperson: The Hon. (Name), House of Representatives, Washington, DC 20515, Dear (Mr., Ms., or Mrs.) (Name). The best close is Sincerely yours. Note that street addresses, building names, and room numbers are unnecessary.

5. Cizik, 95.

6. John W. Montgomery, "The Limits of Christian Influence," Current Religious Thought Column in *Christianity Today*, 23 January 1981, 60.

7. Galatians 5:19-23.

8. Leviticus 25:10.

9. John 8:32.

10. Forest D. Montgomery, *One Nation Under God* (Wheaton, Ill.: NAE, 1986), 19.

11. Psalm 33:12.

12. Benjamin Weiss, *God in American History*, (Grand Rapids: Zondervan, 1966), 92.

13. Genesis 1:26f.

14. Proverbs 6:16f.

15. Amos 5:24.

16. Charles W. Colson, "Putting Justice Together Again," *Justice Report*, Winter 1990.

17. Robert Holland, "Racial Rigged Job Test Scores," *Washington Times*, 7 June 1990, F1.

18. Jack Anderson and Dale Van Atta, "Parents Who Skip Town," *Washington Post*, 20 May 1990.

19. Justice Fellowship, an affiliate of Charles Colson's Prison Fellowship, seeks "to restore balance to the criminal justice system by focusing on reforms which address the needs of victims." While JF believes that society must be protected from violent offenders, it argues that "non-dangerous offenders should be sentenced to restitution and community service programs rather than prison." JF's address: Justice Fellowship, P.O. Box 17181, Washington, DC 20041-0181.

20. 1 Timothy 5:8.

21. William Raspberry, "Family Stories," *Washington Post*, 29 July 1990.

22. Proverbs 29:18.

Chapter Five

Changing the Politicians Themselves

Despite constant grassroots efforts, some politicians will prove impossibly stubborn when it comes to certain issues. Their minds simply will not be changed.

Fortunately, we need not be perpetually frustrated when, for example, a senator's voting record shows that he inevitably prefers a woman's "right" to an abortion over protecting the unborn. Nor are we limited to gnashing our teeth when a congresswoman's vote reveals that she prefers gay rights over a religious institution's right to practice its faith.

Under the Constitution, when we are unable to change our office-holders' minds, we can change the politicians themselves. Doing that, through elections, is not as difficult as most people think it is, and it would be a whole lot easier if more citizens were willing to get involved.

It comes as a great surprise to most Americans that our nation's political course has so often swung on narrowly decided elections. Did you know that Richard Nixon came very close to defeating John F. Kennedy for the presidency in 1960? Or that Jimmy Carter just barely turned Gerald Ford out of the White House in 1976?

Since we can never know for certain when our state or congressional district vote may be very close, our interests can be defeated by the narrowest of margins. The way to prevent that is by significant, personal campaign involvement.

"Significant" campaigning could be something as simple as putting a bumper sticker on your car. It could also be much more than that—and easy to do, fun, and of great consequence.

Who wins elections? The most attractive candidates? The candidates whose political views make the most sense? The candidates with the largest campaign treasuries? The answer is: None of the above.

Appealing and articulate candidates with engaging personalities have no automatic lock on election victories. If you haven't sat recently in the gallery with the full House of Representatives in session, look through the *Almanac of American Politics* at the pictures of the members of Congress. It is not being unkind to suggest that few of the men would be matinee idols and few of the women beauty queens. But then, few of the general population would be, either. Those ordinary people who win elections are a cross-section of the rest of us. You might wonder how some of them could win with strange-sounding names, names practically impossible to spell. No, the victors are not all a public relations firm's packaging dream.

Intelligent candidates, with solid grasp of the issues and a political approach with common sense, do not necessarily emerge victorious either. Some incumbents get away with voting one way in Washington and talking another way at home. Most citizens haven't the foggiest notion of the true voting record of their representative or senators, and thus can easily have the wool pulled over their eyes. The picture of a voting public eagerly standing by to throw bodily into office the candidate with genuine wisdom is too ludicrous to discuss.

Nor are affluent candidates, whether personally wealthy or successful in fund raising, necessarily guaranteed victory. In Wisconsin in 1980, former congressman Robert Kasten found himself in a three-way primary battle for the Republican nomination for the United States Senate. One of his opponents raised and spent $700,000. Another amassed an incredible $1.3 million. Kasten, however, won the nomination with campaign expenditures of only $70,000, and went on to win the Senate seat in November.

One rare exception to the minimizing of money should be noted. On occasion, a party cannot find a viable, willing challenger, yet wishes to field a candidate. That happened in 1990 when new York Governor Mario Cuomo seemed invincible. Republican leaders then "gave" the nomination to a politically unknown Pierre Rinfret, largely because he was willing to pour large amounts of his personal wealth into what others saw as a kamikaze run against Cuomo.

Don't misunderstand. Being attractive, astute, and affluent are not disadvantages for a political candidate. Certainly, being lackluster, stupid, or impoverished is nothing to brag about. It's just that good qualities are not the key to success. Organization is.

Other things being equal, the candidate backed by the best organization of volunteers is far more often than not going to win. Bob Kasten should take a bow, because his organizational strategy for victory has become legendary. Professional campaign training seminars teach "The Kasten Plan."

For his congressional races, Kasten built a campaign organization with a traditional chairman and manager at the top. Dividing his district into regions, the campaign produced a staff of volunteers with a Kasten chairperson in every precinct—the basic, vital unit of politics. Every precinct has a polling place for elections and serves as a clearly defined area for political operations.

After careful analysis of the voting records in the various precincts, Kasten's campaign set a challenging but realistic vote total goal for each precinct, and it was the job of his volunteer to meet or exceed that goal. Thus, hundreds of men and women accepted the responsibility to put Kasten into office, did what was necessary to "sell" voters on their man, identified Kasten supporters, and one way or another got them to the polls on election day. Their combined efforts put him over the top.

No wonder, then, that in 1980 Kasten took his party's Senate nomination when one of his opponents spent nineteen times the money he did, and the other ten times. Ironically, in the years between his service in the House and his entry into the Senate, Kasten ran for governor of Wisconsin and was defeated. In that one gubernatorial primary, the decision was made to short-cut his own strategy. Only that once did Kasten not use "The Kasten Plan," and only that once did he lose.

When it comes to elections, two kinds of organizations combine to assist candidates: political parties and campaign organizations.

Always in place are the two national parties, with state, county, and local organizational structures.[1] Each has a logical assignment: The national party to elect a president every four years; the state organization to elect those who run statewide, such as governor, attorney general, and U.S. senators; the county party to elect county commissioners; and so on. Parties are comprised of an organization of officers and leaders, their elected officials, grassroots activists who give time and money, and voters who identify with that party and generally support its candidates.

The other organization is the one developed by the candidate. It is always wise to build one's own organization, rather than to rely solely on the party. Party workers may put more effort into another race. They may go all out for a glamorous gubernatorial nominee, but give only half-hearted effort to their steady congressional nominee. On the other hand, it would be a foolish candidate who did not cultivate party leaders warmly, letting it be known that party support is crucial for his campaign. His volunteers, he will assure them, always stand ready to help the party.

One congressman told me that just three hundred

people, deeply committed to a campaign, would be enough to put a candidate in Congress.[2] I built such a committee for my campaign in 1976—or I thought I had. We recruited many friends who had never before participated in a campaign, always outlining the sort of work that would be required in the final weeks, and the kind of commitment we were counting on. Slowly we built the list, never adding names just to reach the magic number.

Our campaign manager was thrilled to see a list like that. He promptly mailed a letter to our committee, describing ways they could help and asking that a questionnaire be returned. When the response was disappointingly slim, Lynne volunteered to call everyone on the committee who had not yet responded. Before the campaign was over, she called through that list four times. Not even the candidate's wife could prod those friends into action.

For whatever reasons, our committee of three hundred on paper turned out to be about one-third that size in active campaigning. The majority of our "committed" friends found no convenient time to give us a hand, or no suitable assignment. If any one factor was responsible for my loss, it was the failure of my campaign organization to live up to its potential. Other evangelical candidates have reported similar problems.

By contrast, the most common route to office is reflected in the following story. In 1964, a young Denver area businessman's presidential preference was strong enough that he placed a political poster in a window. As he was cutting his grass one Saturday morning, a passing driver saw the sign, hit his brakes, rolled down his window and commented about the Goldwater poster. In the ensuing conversation, he ruefully reported that Republicans hadn't been able to staff that precinct, and wondered if this new acquaintance might be willing to help. Never involved in politics before, Ted agreed to help, provided that he could have some guidance. He soon learned the ropes.

A couple of years later, Ted walked into his legislative district assembly a few minutes late. Suddenly there was silence and everyone looked at him. The chairman cleared his throat and took the plunge: "Ted, we've just been talking about you. As you know, nobody's come forward to run for the state legislature in this district. You've done a good job for the party in your precinct, we think you'd be a good candidate, and we frankly want you to run. How about it?"

Startled, Ted said precisely what most of us would have said: "Who, me?" That was the beginning. As an evangelical Christian, Ted prayed for God's leading in his decision—and it put him in the state legislature that year, even though his district's party registration was two-to-one against him. From there, he would shortly move up to the state senate where he serves today as senate president, one of the most important positions in Colorado politics. Moreover, in 1978 and 1986 he won the Republican nomination for governor.

If Ted Strickland had refused to do basic precinct work in 1964, today only his family might know him in Colorado. Ted's willingness to invest a few hours in politics when he was young opened the door for him to run twice for governor, and to be one of Colorado's prominent political leaders.

It isn't surprising that both Democrats and Republicans find their candidates within their own ranks. Friendships, IOU's, and a certain logical progression make it possible for party insiders to predict who will come along as nominees for the next decade. You can almost see the line forming. It is so unusual for a party to look beyond its own ranks to find a candidate that very few examples come to mind. Here's one. After World War II, both parties sought to cultivate war hero General Dwight Eisenhower as a presidential candidate. The Republicans snared him and thus controlled the White House for eight years.

The exception proves the rule. If evangelicals are frustrated that comparatively few fellow-believers are in

office, they should ask how many of their people are
sufficiently involved in party politics that they, like Ted
Strickland, may one day be running for governor. How
many serve in the state legislature, or as party county
chairman, from which they are well positioned to run for
Congress? Evangelicals, like anybody else, need to earn the
right to ask their party to entrust them with a nomination
for high office.

There's a lot to be learned from a quick look at some
fascinating presidential and congressional election
statistics. These are not boring numbers. For those who
care about change, they make a very encouraging case for
political involvement.

Presidential Elections

Because the three presidential elections of the '80s have
been about as one-sided as an earthquake, most Americans
do not realize that in several prior elections this century,
the winner came close to being defeated.

1976 provides a sterling example. Jimmy Carter
defeated Gerald Ford by an electoral vote of 297-240, but
if Ford had carried Ohio with its 25 votes (in the '70s),
and Hawaii with its four, he would have won by a hair's
breadth—269-268. Such figures would be statistically
meaningless except for the close margins in both those
states. It would have required less than 5,600 switched
votes in Ohio and 3,700 in Hawaii to reverse the national
outcome, allowing Ford to remain as president.

Richard Nixon became president in 1968 with a
popular vote edge of only 510,000 out of 72 million votes
cast, although his electoral college margin was substantial.
Of course, it is theoretically possible to win the presidency
in the electoral college while losing the popular vote. The
more interesting Nixon election, statistically, was his loss
eight years earlier to John F. Kennedy. The 1960 electoral
vote was 303-219.

If, however, Illinois and Missouri had gone Nixon's
way, plus any one of the following three—Nevada, New

Mexico, or South Carolina—Kennedy would have lost by at least 260-262. Again, such speculation would mean little, except for the close votes in all those states. Less than six thousand needed to be switched in Illinois—but many historians now believe that the election was stolen from Nixon in Illinois, where Chicago Mayor Richard Daley's famed Democratic machine saw to it that the tombstones voted, early and often. In Missouri, less than five thousand needed to shift. With under thirteen hundred shifting in Nevada, less than twelve hundred shifting in New Mexico, or less than five thousand shifting in South Carolina, Nixon would have picked up the added three, four, or eight electoral votes necessary to put him over the top.

In 1916, before the days of computer projections, the nation waited much, much longer for ballots to be tabulated. Finally, it came down to California. If that West Coast state had gone Republican, Charles Evans Hughes would have become president (instead of later returning to the Supreme Court in 1930 as chief justice). As it was, by that one state margin, Woodrow Wilson became president during World War I, and assumed the weighty responsibilities of both conducting the war and developing post-war policies.

In any or all of those elections, if the losing party had a gifted forecaster, it would have been no trick at all to rush reinforcements into the key states, pick up a few thousand votes, and turn the election around. Since only God has foreknowledge and omniscience, however, the parties must be guided by polling data, applying extra pressure in close states in hopes that the organizations will do their absolute best. That best is dependent on the hard work of volunteers.

Now for a candid question. Have evangelicals historically been much of a factor in the presidential campaign process?

For the most recent four elections, the answer is yes, but it is no for most preceding elections. While no political or church leader can create or control an evangelical voting bloc, nevertheless millions of evangelical Christians have collectively produced such a bloc by tracking certain issues, studying the parties, looking over the candidates, and voting accordingly. It began back in 1976, when evangelicals played the major part in putting Jimmy Carter into the Oval Office. They most certainly accounted for Carter's margins of victory in closely contested states, when great numbers departed from habitual Republican presidential voting patterns to cast a vote for a fellow-believer, a Democrat.

The Reagan-Bush team did not forget their 1980 evangelical supporters as they looked toward '84. When 52.6 percent of Americans of voting age cast their ballots—reversing a declining presidential turnout of twenty years—Ronald Reagan ran up 525 electoral votes, the highest total ever.[3] CBS exit polls indicated that 78 percent of the white evangelical vote had helped Reagan build the fifth largest popular vote margin in history.

This second consecutive Republican victory prompted Rep. Pat Schroeder (D-CO) to suggest in a speech, "There are three things we Democrats need to do to recapture the White House." Pausing for effect, she finished, "Unfortunately, nobody knows what they are." The party's new national chairman had an idea for one smart step. He yanked official standing from the Gay and Lesbian Caucus—one among several evidences that the Democrats had not attempted to attract the evangelical vote in 1984.

Evangelical religious broadcaster Pat Robertson sought the Republican presidential nomination in 1988. While his showing was significant, and while he helped to focus the debate, he was never able to capture the evangelical community as his base, let alone find substantial support elsewhere among the electorate. The media generally expressed surprise on learning that, in soundings of evangelical leadership, NAE several times found Robertson only the fourth choice among Republican contenders.

Many felt that his campaign was just not feasible—that America would not put an ordained minister in the Oval Office, even if he had turned back his ordination credentials. Others were uncomfortable with some of Robertson's theology or public utterances.

Before and after winning the Republican nomination, George Bush cultivated evangelical leaders in a number of small meetings in the nation's capital, some in his White House office and others at his vice presidential residence. He listened to their counsel, echoed many of their convictions in his convention acceptance speech in New Orleans, and pulled 82 percent of the white evangelical vote in his near-landslide electoral college victory of 426-112. As a voting bloc, evangelicals gave Bush his largest identifiable margin of support.

In a White House meeting a month later, I told the president-elect why I thought he had won such a victory: While his campaign train ran on the track of peace and prosperity, there was a third rail that delivered the power, as in Washington's Metro subway system. That rail was traditional values. Not only evangelicals, but millions of others found those values appealing.

Earlier, evangelical leaders recommended to Bush three possible vice presidential choices that would send the right signal to their constituents: Senator Bill Armstrong of Colorado, Congressman Jack Kemp of New York, or Governor John Ashcroft of Missouri. The choice of Indiana Senator Dan Quayle took everyone by surprise, but the evangelicals' first reaction was positive. Quayle held their value-system and shared their faith. As the media pummeled Dan Quayle unmercifully, the Christian news magazine *World* ran this little piece in an article about him:

> He struggled with his grades from the day he entered school. He carried the rap of a pampered child past the time he was no longer one. Even in his majority his mother did everything she could to see her son avoid exposure to military action; when it

was unavoidable, she made certain he went in style. He rode off to war as a correspondent in as much splendor as a troopship could afford. . . . His valet even packed a high powered spyglass for viewing the battles from a safe distance.

His heroics on the battlefield were unofficial, tinted with a shade of circumstance and his own embellishments. Returning from the battlefield, he enjoyed only fleeting glory and popularity, and was treated mercilessly by his peers in the House of Commons.

But privilege, where it has touched on military experience, existed long before Winston Churchill headed off to cover the Boer War.[4]

I do not assume that Dan Quayle will develop into a Winston Churchill; nor should the media and others assume, based on his early life, that he may not. In any case, by their overwhelming vote, evangelicals put him into office along with the 41st president of the United States, George Herbert Walker Bush.

Senate Elections

It is tempting to write concerning a number of classic, close Senate contests, like New Hampshire's in 1974 with its two-vote margin. Let me instead mention just one. It was the 1984 Republican senate primary in Texas, and the actual vote totals of the three candidates were 455,768, 454,807, and 454,497. Former Democratic Rep. Kent Hance topped the Republican list with his 33.4 percent plurality.[5] A few more friends helping, a few more contributions, and either of the finishers with 33.3 percent each could have grabbed the top spot.

The biggest Senate election story in a quarter century developed in 1980. The combined election of Ronald Reagan and the unexpected turnover in the U.S. Senate recorded 7.8 on the Richter Scale of Washington's political seismograph. Going into election day, the Senate remained controlled by the Democrats, as it had been for twenty-six consecutive years. They had fifty-nine seats to the Republicans' forty-one.[6] As the votes were tallied that night, twelve seats shifted, every one from the Democratic into the Republican column.

Republicans were ecstatic. By 53-47, they would now be the committee chairs and appoint two-thirds of the committee staffs. They would be able to assist President Reagan to jam on government's brakes and make a hard right turn, if not a U-turn, and start cutting back on both government spending and federal taxation. Remember, it was evangelicals who provided the final increment of votes that made the historic turn possible—an unforgettable manifestation of political power. A remarkable new day had dawned in U.S. politics.

Equally remarkable were the margins that made possible this major upset. Eleven Senate elections were won with 51 percent or less of the vote, and only two of those were Democrat wins, Hart (CO) and Leahy (VT) with 51 percent each. Nine of the closest elections went to Republicans. Winning 45-44 percent in a three-way race was D'Amato (NY). Barely squeaking through with 50 percent were Goldwater (AZ), Symms (ID), and East (NC). At 51 percent were Denton (AL), Hawkins (FL), Mattingly (GA), Specter (PA), and Kasten (WI). Two more Republican victories were achieved with 52 percent of the vote.

The moral of this story? If they had only known, volunteers being the key to victory, the Democrats would surely have put enough troops into several of those very close contests to foil the Republican takeover. But they didn't. On such margins history hangs.

Republicans kept control of the Senate in 1982, but barely. Of thirty-four Senate races, fourteen saw winners with 52 percent or less of the vote. A shift of less than thirty-five thousand votes in Vermont, Rhode Island, Missouri, Wyoming, and Nevada would have given Democrats those five seats, allowing them to wrest control from the GOP. But it didn't happen.

The tables were turned in 1986, when Democrats

regained control of the Senate in the middle of Ronald Reagan's second term. That marked the death-knell of his effectiveness with Congress. This time the seven closest elections were all won by Democrats. Senator Conrad won with 50 percent. Senators Shelby (AL), Cranston (CA), Wirth (CO), Fowler (GA), Reid (NV), and Adams (WA) all topped out with 51 percent. Now Republicans had the unpleasant task of second-guessing themselves and asking, "What if? . . ."

This might be a good time to answer a question thoughtful evangelicals often ask: Is it possible for a genuinely Christian candidate to win in the political major leagues? Without question, the answer is yes. There are many examples in Congress, but consider Senator William L. Armstrong's 1984 campaign in Colorado. The senator had sponsored the congressional resolution making 1983 The Year of the Bible, and television spots were then being shown in his state which asked, "Is being a U.S. Senator the most important thing in Bill Armstrong's life? No. His relationship to God is." Viewers were invited to send for a book about their relationship to God.

Political advisors urged Armstrong to pull the spots from the air, but this NAE "Layman of the Year" said no. He insisted on doing what he believed God wanted, and letting the chips fall where they might. His opponent, Lieutenant Governor Nancy Dick, charged that "This man wants to force his beliefs down your throat," and those beliefs, she hastened to add, included a pro-life position as well as his personal faith. Despite that, Armstrong did better even than President Reagan in Colorado and was reelected with 64 percent of the vote. Accuser Nancy Dick's 36 percent was the lowest percentage ever for a Democrat in a Colorado Senate race.

House Elections

Wisecracks about Congress are common. What is uncommon is a willingness to work to alter the 435 member House of Representatives. Change must come one congressional district at a time. Evangelicals must take responsibility for the district in which they live.

Since 1966, except for the Watergate year of '74, House elections have seen over 90 percent of members seeking reelection. Political recidivism has been on the increase. In '86, 383 of 395 representatives running for another term were successful—an impressive 97 percent rate of return. On the other hand, forty seats were being vacated and almost 10 percent of House elections were targeting open seats. In '88, the House success rate for incumbents fighting to keep their seats was over 98 percent.

Such statistics seem terribly discouraging to challengers and to those thinking of joining their campaigns. On the other hand, after the '88 elections a full 63 percent of all current representatives had entered Congress in the '80s. There is a significant turnover during every election cycle, whether of members leaving to run for other office (usually the Senate or governor), retiring, or dying.

Never is there a shortage of close House elections. Take 1984. In Idaho, a Democratic challenger unseated incumbent George Hausen by 67 votes out of 202,000. A Republican captured an open seat in Utah by just 143 of 209,000 votes. In Pennsylvania, incumbent Bob Edgar successfully defended his seat by a razor-thin 481 of 248,000 votes, but the defeated Curt Weldon captured that seat in '86 when Edgar ran unsuccessfully for the Senate. It took until April to determine that Rep. Frank McCloskey had held onto his Indiana seat by just 4 votes out of 234,000.

Look at 1986. Three Republican incumbents narrowly won their battle to stay in Congress: Howard Coble by 81 out of 145,000 in North Carolina; John Hiler by 166 out of 152,000 in Indiana; and Arlan Stangeland by 211 out of 188,000 in Minnesota. Former professional basketball player Tom McMillen (D) won an open seat by 510 out of 129,000, incidentally becoming the tallest member of Congress. The significantly lower district vote totals in '86 compared to '84 are not difficult to explain. Voters show more interest in a presidential election year, and 1984 was such a year.

Finally, look at 1988. Incumbent Denny Smith (R) barely survived by a 707 vote margin, with 222,000 cast, in Oregon. Challenger Craig James unseated a senior Democrat incumbent by 732 out of 250,000 votes in Florida. Jolene Unsoeld (D) captured an open seat by 618 out of 218,000 in Washington.

Since it is impossible to foresee when an election may be close, wise evangelicals will become part of campaigns either for an appreciated incumbent or for an admirable challenger. The conventional wisdom is that challengers should always be willing to run at least twice. Gains in experience, name recognition, and organizational effectiveness could put your candidate in Congress the second time around, if not the first.[7]

Amateur political strategists need to be reminded of another critical feature on the political landscape. After each decade's official U.S. census, congressional districts around the nation are reapportioned, so that the various states get their share according to population. The idea is that congressional districts be as nearly equal in population as possible. Once it is known, for example, that California's House delegation will increase from forty-five to fifty-two in 1992, political leaders will draw new congressional district boundaries.

State government controls that process. Where one party has the governor and a majority in both houses of the legislature, the likelihood that these lines will be gerrymandered to that party's advantage are approximately 100 percent. The time-honored practice of gerrymandering, which ignores natural geographical boundaries in favor of political considerations, comes from Elbridge Gerry, a signer of the Declaration of Independence and governor of Massachusetts. When a district drawn to his instructions looked like a salamander, some wit combined Gerry's name with the salamander's—which makes for an interesting trivia question in the late twentieth century.

The redistricting process in fifty states explains why, after the '84 election,[8] the percentage of Democrats and Republicans in the House did not match the national vote. Nationwide, Democrats won 43 million congressional votes while Republicans took 39 million. That's 52.4 percent to 47.6 percent. Yet the Democrats, with 260 members to the Republicans' 175, held 58 percent of all the House seats.

California shows what flagrant gerrymandering can do. In 1984, 4,228,000 congressional ballots were cast for Republicans across the state, to 4,210,000 for Democrats. Nevertheless, Democrats sent twenty-seven Representatives to the House while the GOP sent a meager eighteen. With only 49.9 percent of the popular vote, Democrats controlled 60 percent of the House seats. Their 27-18 edge had not changed by the end of the decade.

Now you know why the national party committees invest as heavily as they do in their state organizations. The party that loses the bulk of the redistricting struggles will be behind the eight-ball in Congress for a decade to come. Astute evangelicals will see the folly of ignoring state level politics to focus only on national.

The all-time close election among state legislatures came in 1978, when the Pennsylvania House of Representatives found each party controlling 101 seats, with the remaining seat deadlocked at 8,551 votes. It took a recount to break the tie and award the seat—by fourteen votes. You never know.

Here's a nearly incredible key legislative victory. State Rep. Penny Pullen of Illinois apparently lost by thirty-one votes in her 1990 primary battle against a one-issue, pro-abortion challenger, funded by the National Abortion Rights Action League.

An evangelical, Penny was an acknowledged leader of the pro-life forces in Illinois. When a recount produced an exact tie, a state-sponsored coin flip awarded the seat to her opponent, but Pullen took the matter to the Illinois

Supreme Court, arguing that the intent of some of the previously rejected ballots could be determined. Discovering that eight of the thirty ballots had partial holes in the punch card ballots, the court gave her opponent just one of those and Penny seven—and the nomination.

To wrap up this chapter, I point to a president and a would-be president to demonstrate how a comparatively unimportant election here or there can trigger events that channel the flow of history.

Lyndon Johnson "won" his first primary election for the U.S. Senate in 1948, by 87 votes out of more than 988,000 cast. In Texas in those days, the Democratic primary victory guaranteed a Senate victory in November. It now seems clear that Johnson raised the art of campaign fraud to new heights that year, as he demonstrably stole the election.[9] By a mere eighty-seven vote margin, LBJ put himself into position one day to be president. Never a senator, never a president. Once in the Oval Office, Johnson would fail to conclude the war in Vietnam but succeed in passing the massive spending programs of his "Great Society"—programs creating entitlements that have much to do with today's budget deficits and huge national debt.

In 1962, George S. McGovern was elected to the U.S. Senate from South Dakota, by a margin of less than one vote per precinct. Like Johnson, never a senator, never a presidential nominee. In 1972, the liberal McGovern became the Democrats' choice to run against Richard Nixon. As it turned out, McGovern was far too liberal for the American people and Nixon trounced him. But suppose that the Democrats had nominated a more moderate candidate that year and that Nixon had been defeated. Then the nation would not have been dragged through the anguish of Watergate nor forced to witness the resignation of her president. But history worked out another way—hinging on a narrow Senate victory ten years before in the relatively obscure state of South Dakota.[10]

Voters determined the political fortunes of Johnson, McGovern, and all the others in this chapter. But it was the campaign volunteers who persuaded them how to vote and who, through such narrow victories, literally shaped history.

Notes

1. See Appendix II for a list of national and state party offices.

2. A strange "coincidence" occurred in church the following Sunday. The pastor preached from the Old Testament account of a judge named Gideon (Judges 7). Because God did not want Israel to boast that her superior military forces had beaten Midian, he instructed Gideon to send home any who were fearful. A force of thirty-two thousand was thus reduced to ten thousand. There were still too many, so, on instruction, Gideon retained only those who drank from a brook by cupping their hands to their mouths, reducing his force to three hundred. Using God's strategy, those three hundred routed the superior forces of Midian. I slipped a note to Lynne during the service: "We're going to build a committee of three hundred."

3. Franklin Roosevelt deserves an asterisk for his 523 votes in 1936. There were only forty-eight states in those days, and he carried all but the eight electoral votes from Maine and Vermont.

4. "With Polish, Maybe—J. Winston Quayle?" *World*, 26 September 1989, 9.

5. Unfortunately for Hance, he lost a two-man runoff a few weeks later. That race was particularly interesting to me because Hance and I were members of the same church in suburban Virginia.

6. Technically, the Democrats had fifty-eight seats and Virginia's Harry Byrd was an Independent. Byrd always voted with the Democrats to organize the Senate, however, so I include him in their number here.

7. I followed that conventional wisdom when I geared up to run again in 1978, but before the campaign really got rolling we pulled back with an eye on '80 instead. Long before that date arrived, however, NAE called me to Washington.

8. *Congressional Quarterly*'s research service could not provide comparable statistics for 1988.

9. Robert A. Caro, *The Years of Lyndon Johnson: Means of Ascent.* (New York: Knopf, 1990).

10. Except for those who live there—from whom I expect to get some choice letters.

Chapter Six

A Decade of Changing the Political Landscape

In its infinite wisdom, the Internal Revenue Service in August 1978 provoked a reaction that led to unprecedented evangelical political involvement in the 1980s. The IRS proposed a number of regulations for private schools which presumed them to be racist—and no longer qualified for tax-exempt status—if their student bodies did not contain an "adequate" percentage of minority students (based on their local communities). Had the scheme gone through, alleged "white flight academies" would probably have been forced to close their doors.

The regulations comprised nothing less than a threat to put a large segment of the Christian school movement out of business. When the IRS scheduled December dates for public comments, I testified. The IRS had to be stopped, lest faceless bureaucrats label hundreds of Christian schools as segregationist. They would be presumed guilty until they could somehow prove themselves innocent. That's not the way American justice is supposed to work.

The action sparked a storm of protest, with hearings extended to four days. One testimony about a Hebrew school located in a 50 percent Hispanic Miami neighborhood blew the IRS' assumptions to smithereens. How could the IRS suspect that school of discriminating against Hispanics, most of whom were Roman Catholic? Few of them were likely to seek admission to a Jewish school.

Should the IRS force Jews to recruit Hispanics, thus making the federal government indirectly responsible for Jewish evangelism? Try fitting that into the First Amendment.

The impact of the collective testimony—backed by a mass of protest from Christians across the country—was overwhelming. The IRS postponed implementation of its proposals and, in 1980, Congress passed the Ashbrook-Dornan amendments which prohibited the IRS from yanking tax-exempt status from religious schools. If the IRS had not seen the light, at least it had felt the heat. That's often how things work in politics.

Key to the victory were the grassroots objections of thousands of Christian citizens. To produce future pressure on the IRS, Congress, or the White House, it was obvious that evangelicals needed reliable information about issues affecting them in Washington. I myself had been "out there" for years and would have been willing to pay a king's ransom for a trustworthy newsletter—an evangelical equivalent of the *Kiplinger Washington Letter* for businessmen. That's why the monthly *NAE Washington Insight*[1] was born in March 1979. For twelve years our monthly newsletter has been providing inside information and interpreting what government is doing, or threatening to do.

The Birth of the Pro-Family Movement

It was the mid-point of the Carter Administration when I had come to Washington. I discovered that most of the religious community in the capital felt it was more difficult to establish contact in the Carter White House than with any administration since Eisenhower's. I theorized that the president's staff wanted to de-emphasize Carter's widely publicized "born again" faith. The fewer religious leaders around him, the less people would be reminded of his faith, already too prominent for certain staffers' liking.

In any case, things began to change in the summer of '79, after Carter brought Southern Baptist minister Robert Maddox to his White House staff as a speechwriter, and then assigned him liaison duties to the religious community. All his skills would be needed for a major conflict brewing during Carter's final year. A special White House program was about to galvanize Christians and others into the pro-family movement.

When we first got wind of the White House Conference on the Family, that was its name. But by 1980 it had been renamed the White House Conference on Families. By this subtle shift, liberal social scientists could avoid the implication that there was a traditionally definable entity known as "the family"—persons related by blood, marriage, or adoption. That, of course, is the biblical definition. Conference planners wanted to install the American Home Economics Society's definition: "People who share the same living or cooking quarters and have a long-term commitment to each other." The sky would have been the limit on such "family" groupings.

Evangelicals were troubled, but at the same time encouraged that some of their leaders secured presidential appointment to the conference's final meetings. While pro-family forces did succeed at many points, a composite of positions adopted at those meetings formed a liberal social agenda, in some ways anti-family. To implement them would have required large amounts of federal dollars. Fortunately, the issue became moot when Jimmy Carter was defeated for reelection. Ronald Reagan was hardly going to carry out the liberals' agenda.

Born-again Candidates

There was one political mistake evangelical voters would not be able to repeat in 1980. In the past they might have voted for a presidential candidate solely on the basis of a common Christian faith. Not this time. Incumbent President Jimmy Carter, Republican challenger Ronald Reagan, and independent John B. Anderson all identified themselves as evangelicals. While the ultimate, error-free evaluation can only be made by God, each one seemed to have a credible profession of faith.

Back in 1976, Jimmy Carter's unabashed acknowledgment

of his born-again Christian faith escaped no one's notice. It may have helped him capture the Democratic presidential nomination, partial proof that he was the most conservative candidate in the field. And it brought evangelical Christianity into the limelight, especially through *Newsweek*'s "Year of the Evangelical" cover article. UPI reporter Wesley Pippert analyzed Carter as making a unique attempt to be a servant-leader, within his concept of the New Testament idea of servant. He was a strong family man and dedicated to peace.

Notwithstanding his incumbent's advantage and four years experience in the world's toughest job, Carter was not running strong. His track record in coping with economic and energy problems was poor, and his foreign policy skills were mocked by the Iranian hostage situation. Among evangelicals, there was puzzlement and even disillusionment. Did they not have a right to expect that a fellow-believer would share their views on abortion and school prayer? His explanation that his sincerely held view of separation of church and state did not allow his spiritual convictions to shape his political positions would not wash. Further, why had he failed to include evangelicals in top-level positions in his administration?

Republican nominee Ronald Reagan was running on his track record as governor of California, our most heavily populated state. He had created a surplus from the state's deficit and eliminated a great deal of welfare fraud. Almost instinctively he identified with many of the moral and spiritual concerns of evangelicals, such as the sanctity of human life, the importance of returning voluntary prayer to the nation's schools, and the value of biblical morality. He convinced evangelicals that he would include qualified persons from their ranks in his administration. Reagan's personal faith was not as clearly expressed as that of Carter and Anderson, but it did appear genuine.

Moderately liberal congressman John Anderson entered the competition for the Republican nomination in June but, failing there, became an independent candidate.

Anderson's 1964 designation as the National Association of Evangelicals' "Layman of the Year" was included in his official biography, but he would never have been granted that recognition in 1980. A gifted leader, his peers had voted him the second most persuasive orator in the House. He admirably used his rhetorical skills to swing the crucial votes that passed fair housing legislation in 1968.

Carter's campaign practically indicted Anderson with introducing a constitutional amendment to make Christianity the official faith of the nation in 1961, 1963, and again in 1965. Anderson now repudiated that action as immature. Many of his social views had moved so far to the left that evangelicals were left shaking their heads. It seemed incredible that Anderson cosponsored gay rights legislation and supported unrestricted abortion rights, to the embarrassment of his evangelical denomination.[2]

Evangelicals were forced to make a thoughtful choice in this election. Not only did the dramatically divergent positions of Carter, Reagan, and Anderson demand careful evaluation, but a formidable new entity made its debut in presidential politics in 1980.

The new religious right saw evangelicals as a huge bloc of generally unmotivated voters. Surveys showed that these religious folk were more conservative than the general population in matters of economics and national defense. How could they be activated to add votes that would put conservatives in the win column? It dawned on new right strategists that issues like abortion, prayer in schools, and pornography would be of great moral concern to Bible-believing Christians, once they were informed. They went after the evangelical vote.

Meanwhile, the Republican Party had been cultivating evangelical leaders. I was part of a small cadre of leaders who had been getting acquainted with potential Republican presidential nominees—and, eventually with the Democratic nominee, President Jimmy Carter. In August 1979 we met with John Connally on his Texas ranch. Then followed fall meetings with Ronald Reagan,

Sen. Howard Baker (R-TN), and Rep. Phil Crane (R-IL). In early spring we met George Bush in Chicago.

During the 1980 National Religious Broadcasters convention, twelve of us were invited to the White House for breakfast with Jimmy Carter. The president remained for forty minutes of frank discussion, better than the fifteen pledged by his staff.

As promised, Republicans did indeed pitch their platform to evangelicals. They endorsed efforts to restore voluntary prayer to public schools, supported a constitutional amendment banning abortion on demand, and favored tuition-tax credits that would allow parents a realistic possibility of educating their children in Christian schools. In a highly controversial section, they even pledged to nominate federal judges who opposed abortion. Democrats, on the other hand, took opposing positions, even endorsing the drive for homosexual rights and against discrimination on the basis of sexual orientation. Support of gay rights was not calculated to attract biblical Christians.

As everyone knows, by the time Ronald Reagan arrived at the Republican convention in Detroit, the only suspense was his choice of a running mate. President Carter easily outdistanced Sen. Ted Kennedy (D-MA) for renomination. The election in November promised to be a cliffhanger.

It wasn't. Evangelicals were part of the reason. The nation's political crust shifted massively in 1980, the election shaking the country like a major earthquake. The public heeded the Republican slogan to vote "for a change," and commentators compared Reagan's victory to the dramatic turnabout election of Franklin D. Roosevelt in 1932. Indeed, until then in this century only Alf Landon in 1936 and George McGovern in 1972, among major party candidates, won fewer electoral college votes than did Jimmy Carter in his 489-49 loss. He became only the eighth incumbent to lose a presidential reelection bid.

Talk about changing the political landscape through elections! The United States of America felt the impact of the evangelical voting bloc for the first time. Ever since 1980, we evangelicals have been a force to reckon with.

Millions deserted Carter at the polls, all the while probably regarding him as a decent man, personally honest, and with good intentions. Many of those were the so-called born-again voters who, ironically, probably had been responsible for putting him into the White House in '76.

Disappointed, disillusioned, distanced, or whatever, evangelicals who had once strongly supported Carter switched allegiance. According to the ABC News-Lou Harris survey, the white Baptist vote in the South revealed what happened. In 1976, that vote had preferred Carter to Gerald Ford 56 percent to 43 percent. By 1980, white Southern Baptists preferred Reagan over their own Southern Baptist Sunday school teaching Jimmy Carter by 56 percent to 34 percent.[3] Reading Bob Maddox' book *Preacher in the White House,* I got the feeling that neither he nor Jimmy Carter ever really understood why evangelicals forsook the president. Maybe it is fairer to suggest that they never accepted him.[4]

John Anderson's independent candidacy was not a factor in Carter's loss. *Newsweek*'s "Mr. None-of-the-Above" did tally a vote total larger than the Reagan/Carter differential in fifteen states, but if Carter had carried the 167 electoral votes from all of them, Reagan still would have been elected by 322-216.

Evangelical leaders did not set out to construct an evangelical voting bloc, although some of the new religious right leaders did. When the election's smoke had cleared, the Moral Majority's Jerry Falwell and others minimized the impact of the evangelical vote. The humble stance was strategic. While grander claims might have been justified, they would have sounded an alarm to their opponents.

What was the actual evangelical impact upon the election of Ronald Reagan? A baseball analogy makes sense. If a team wins an 8-7 game, any player on the winning team who scored or batted in a run could technically claim that "his" run furnished the victory margin. On the other hand, that run or RBI would have been in vain without the other runs. Thus, analysts were forced to acknowledge that born-again voters at least batted in a run. With others, they produced the victory.

Disappointment with Reagan

One thing about Reagan disappointed evangelicals. He and Nancy, citing security problems, failed to attend worship services on Sundays. Instead, on weekends they either remained in the White House, helicoptered to Camp David, or flew to their ranch above Santa Barbara. That makes Nancy Reagan's comments about spiritual things, never mentioned publicly before their last summer in office, fascinating. The First Lady addressed a national conference of Youth for Christ in the nation's capital on July 27, 1988:

> My father, who died six years ago, was a brilliant man, an internationally known brain surgeon. He was a person of tremendous self-confidence and intellect. So it is ironic that his spiritual life was influenced by a small, petty event that happened in his childhood. When he was a boy, there was a contest in his Sunday school class. The winner was to receive a Bible. My father knew he'd won the contest, for even then he was totally confident in himself and his abilities. He simply couldn't accept it when the Bible was given to the child of the minister. And in reaction, my father, feeling wronged and disillusioned, allowed no place for faith in his life for the next eighty years.

> He would take my mother and me to church and Sunday school, but he'd leave and come back only when it was time to pick us up. My mother had a very deep religious faith; she read her Bible every night. And it was that deep and abiding faith that helped her tremendously at the end of her life.

> But my father didn't have that and at the end of his life, he was terribly frightened. He was even afraid to

go to sleep for fear he wouldn't wake up. He'd move from chair to chair trying to keep awake and, I guess, alive. I can't tell you how much it hurt to see him this way—this man who had always been so supremely confident and strong in my eyes. My husband wrote him two long letters explaining the encompassing comfort he'd receive if he'd just put himself in the Lord's hands.

I was at the hospital with him, but my father never mentioned to me what happened next; the doctors told me. Two days before he died, he asked to see the hospital chaplain. I don't know what the chaplain did or what he said, but whatever it was, it was the right thing and it gave my father comfort. I noticed he was calmer and not as frightened. When he died the next day, he was at peace, finally. And I was so happy for him. My prayers were answered.[5]

Nancy Reagan's father paid a tragic, lifelong price for a momentary loss of integrity in the church. When we evangelicals seek to bring about change, when we relate to government, media, and even our own constituency, God forbid that we ever do so without absolute integrity.

But for the sovereignty of God, America would not have had much of an opportunity to evaluate the presidency of Ronald Reagan. Remember the intrepid humor of the president, when he scanned the doctors surrounding his hospital gurney, prepared to remove the would-be assassin's bullet? "I hope you're all Republicans!" Chief of the surgical team that day at George Washington University Hospital was Dr. Benjamin Aaron, who later suggested "there was some kind of divine providence riding with that bullet."

Moral Issues

Despite Reagan's early triumphs, evangelicals were restless. Their social concerns had been left on the back burner for the long months while the president and Congress tackled the economy. Toward the end of 1981,

Connecticut Mutual Life released a poll showing that moral issues had gone to the top of the nation's political list. Data disclosed that liberals and conservatives were not as divided as before over traditional matters such as nuclear power, criminal rights, or economics. The survey found the sharpest societal divisions over such issues as homosexuality, marijuana, pornography, and abortion.

During Reagan's first term, the NAE and other religious groups battled for a constitutional amendment to allow prayer in schools, a human life amendment to protect the unborn, tuition tax credit legislation, and against the appointment of an ambassador to the Vatican. Although the votes were not there in Congress, the White House was open to us—in sharp contrast to earlier years. For nearly a year, the White House laid plans for a religious leaders' luncheon with the president. Old lists were considered inadequate. I worked with the White House to adopt criteria for the invitations and then to assemble the guest list. While Catholic, Jewish, and Protestant leaders were of course invited, this time evangelicals were represented at more than token levels. On April 13, 1982, the president hosted more than one hundred national religious leaders, many of whom, like NAE denominational heads and parachurch leaders, were eating in the State Dining Room for the first time. More than half of those invited were evangelicals.

Ronald Reagan, moreover, was willing to go out of his way to address evangelicals. While Presidents Ford in '76 and Reagan in '81 had addressed combined NAE and National Religious Broadcasters conventions in Washington, 1983 marked the first time any president traveled outside Washington to speak to evangelicals. When he did, in Orlando on March 8, 1983, Reagan gave probably the most controversial, and surely most oft-quoted speech of his presidency.[6]

Many commentators took umbrage when the president spoke not of a generic belief in God, but of his faith in the Lord Jesus. *The New York Times'* Anthony Lewis called his speech outrageous and primitive, terming his development of the reality of sin in the world "a simplistic theology— one in fact rejected by most theologians." Lewis failed to note the decline of such liberal theology and the growing sway of its evangelical counterpart.

It was Reagan's application of the doctrine of sin that produced apoplexy in his critics, for this was his "evil empire" speech. He stated that the Soviet communists were "the focus of evil in the modern world," arguing that American military strength was necessary to restrain the "aggressive impulses of an evil empire." He pled for evangelicals to support his strong national defense and deterrence policies and to oppose voices calling for a nuclear freeze.

A String of Victories

Evangelicals began getting into the game in earnest, wanting to change the political landscape by pressing their senators and representatives with letters, phone calls, and personal contacts. Small victories started to appear. In '81, the Family Protection Act was introduced, designed to relieve some of the government imposed pressures on families. One section or another of this omnibus pro-family bill would become law over the next several years.

The following year saw evangelical Dr. C. Everett Koop finally confirmed as Surgeon General of the United States. Without the help of phone calls targeted at members of the Senate Labor and Human Resources Committee on Koop's behalf, his nomination might not have been ratified.

Thanks to a joint resolution passed by Congress, 1983 was signed into law by the president as the "Year of the Bible." Sen. Bill Armstrong (R-CO) gave strong leadership to achieving this national acknowledgment of the place of the Bible in America's heritage.

Finally, within a span of just a few weeks in the summer of 1984, evangelicals reaped a rich legislative harvest. Faithful Christian citizens personally experienced the biblical promise: "Let us not become weary in doing good, for at the proper time we will reap a harvest if we do not give up."[7] Four important pieces of legislation at last bore fruit, each dating back at least three years.

Drunk Driving Legislation

For years Americans had tolerated drunk driving, apparently not realizing the scope of the problem. Twenty-five thousand annual alcohol-related traffic fatalities were almost equivalent to a daily Air Florida crash. (Remember the terrible crash of 1982, when only four persons survived as an ice-laden plane crashed into a bridge over the Potomac? Lynne and I were less than two miles away at the time, crossing another bridge spanning the Potomac in the swirling snowstorm.)

Why the apathy? Why had nothing been done? Perhaps many lawmakers who drank realized they had often gotten away with driving under the influence, and that strong sentences one day might penalize themselves or their friends. We began to editorialize that evangelicals, two-thirds of whom are teetotalers, must take the lead on the issue. When the legislation passed, *Christianity Today* reported comments by a spokesman for Sen. Claiborne Pell (D-RI), chief sponsor of the legislation, that NAE's newsletter "generated a tremendous amount of mail" on the subject. Obviously, we were not the only ones.

Church Audit Procedures Act

In 1981 Mike Coleman visited us in Washington. He and other leaders of the Gulf Coast Community Church in Mobile, Alabama, were troubled about an Internal Revenue Service investigation of their church. The IRS wasn't talking about the reasons for its probe, and eventually it went far beyond the bounds of propriety, even making a brazen request to see all the pastor's personal counseling notes.

At the outset, the church was willing to cooperate, in the spirit of the biblical command to "submit yourselves for the Lord's sake to every authority instituted among men: whether to the king, as the supreme authority, or to governors, who are sent by him to punish those who do wrong and to commend those who do right."[8] But the later demands were impossible. Everyone but the IRS understands that clergy confidentiality is traditionally as sacrosanct as a private lawyer-client relationship. By 1982, the church had finally cleared its name at a cost of more than $100,000 in legal and accounting fees. Sadly, most of the expenditure could have been saved if the IRS had originally informed the church of the basis for its concerns. As it turned out, a disgruntled former member of the church had alleged that church funds were being used for private gain, and had submitted stolen papers as evidence.

Coleman's visit in time led to the drafting of legislation to prevent future harassment of churches, conventions, or associations of churches. It defined the rights and responsibilities of churches in cooperating with IRS investigations, but also placed several requirements upon the IRS. On May 11, 1983, Rep. Mickey Edwards (R-OK) introduced the Church Audit Procedures Act in the House, and simultaneously Sen. Charles Grassley (R-IA) introduced his Senate version. The White House ordered its own Treasury Department not to oppose the bill. Through congressional committee testimonies, marshaling evangelical and other grassroots support, and contacts with members of Congress and their staffs, the CAP Act became the law of the land—attached to the must-pass Senate Deficit Reduction Act. There will be no more IRS "fishing expeditions" in evangelical churches, or in any others.

A New Proposal Perceived as a Social Security Tax on Churches

Back in 1982, government realized that Social Security was paying out $17,000 more per minute than it was taking in (which amounts to nearly $9 billion per year). A National Commission on Social Security Reform was appointed to stop the hemorrhage and to adjust the system for the long term. The president was alarmed enough to talk about a "pending insolvency."

When the Commission made its report, it bundled together many provisions to increase revenues, including a requirement that all employees of non-profit organizations be required to join. Churches would be included, not counting ordained ministers who had always been treated as self-employed for Social Security purposes. Paid church custodians, secretaries, organists and the like would now come under Social Security. For the first time, churches were to be taxed with respect to their religious activity, as distinguished from unrelated business income. It was obvious from the beginning that this provision would never be deleted, because the commission had agreed that the bailout was a package, and that changing at any one point would cause their plan to fail.

Few evangelical churches voiced objections to the new tax. They saw it as a pass-through tax for the ultimate benefit of their employees, rather than an assessment upon the church itself. Several fundamentalist pastors, however, howled in protest. They felt that submitting to this tax would be equivalent to taking money given to the Lord and handing it over to Caesar. So adamant were they, that they spoke of chaining themselves to the White House gates, and they seemed perfectly willing to go to jail for their convictions.

We wanted to head off a church-state confrontation by asking Congress to accommodate the sincere religious beliefs of our fundamentalist friends. An NAE proposal actually became the solution to the problem but, once again, hearings probably would never have been held without considerable complaint coming to Congress from the grassroots. Ultimately, the entire Social Security bailout package was adopted, with a provision avoiding church-state conflict. No minister had to go to jail.

Equal Access

Last, evangelicals won this major religious liberty victory of the decade. In the *Widmar v. Vincent* decision of 1981, the Supreme Court ruled that a state university may not prevent campus organizations from conducting religious services on campus. A ban on religious worship would be a ban on free speech. It would be no violation of the

Establishment Clause of the First Amendment to hold such forums in state university facilities. Religious groups should have "equal access" to those facilities. The court indicated, however, that this decision pertained only to the collegiate level, and that it might rule differently regarding lower level students of "impressionable age."

The Christian Legal Society and NAE were the original allies seeking equal access for high school students. It was ridiculous to think that, at their age, those students needed to be "protected" from discussions of religion, given their wide-ranging high school agendas, or that they might somehow be confused into thinking that a student-sponsored Bible club was state-sponsored because it met in their school building. It seemed that the only kind of speech discriminated against in public schools was religious speech. It was as if a sign was posted at the entrance to America's high schools:

ATTENTION STUDENTS
Your Bill of Rights Forbids
All Voluntary Religious Speech
Among Students in a Group of Two or More
Any Place on this Campus
at Any Time

We intended to establish the civil right to meet in student-initiated clubs for the purposes of religious speech. CLS drew up a model Free Speech Protection Act, first introduced by Sen. Mark Hatfield (R-OR) before the Senate Judiciary Committee. Later his bill took on the name of equal access legislation, like that sponsored by Sen. Jeremiah Denton (R-AL). In the House, Rep. Don Bonker (D-WA) championed the cause. In the summer of '83, CLS director Sam Ericsson and his staff were instrumental in winning the key legal case which would be at the heart of the battle for equal access, *Bender v. Williamsport School District.*

To abbreviate a longer story, we did everything humanly possible to win passage of the Equal Access Act. CLS and

NAE drew up more than twenty pages of questions and answers for members of Congress, so that they could anticipate every possible argument and have convincing answers for colleagues, the press, and the people back home. When the issue came into the courts, we filed friend-of-the-court briefs. Joined in progress by the Baptist Joint Committee on Public Affairs, we worked with the staffs of members.

When the issue reached the floor of the Senate and House, we helped produce a huge grassroots mail and telephone support on Capitol Hill. Especially important in that was Dr. James Dobson, who would invite one or another of us onto his "Focus on the Family" radio program to explain the issue. When he asked his listeners to call, they did, and his is the second most widely syndicated radio program in the nation.

At the end, when equal access had become law, we pulled together a consulting group to draft guidelines for interpreting and implementing the act—including former opponents like the American Civil Liberties Union, the American Jewish Congress, the National Council of Churches, and even People for the American Way, all of whom had a vested interest in seeing that equal access be applied fairly. High school principals reading the guidelines are encouraged to find them clear and balanced, not mere propaganda published by the winning religious groups.

Having worked to the maximum, all of us willingly admit that without God's providence, equal access would never have become law. Let me cite just three instances where it would demand more faith to think that we were "lucky" than to see God's hand at work.

• At the heart of the battle was Lisa Bender, the Pennsylvania high school student who wanted to have a prayer club at Williamsport High School. Before the equal access concept got to Congress, she moved to Kentucky to train to be a missionary. Out of 435 congressional districts in the nation, she just "happened" to move into the district represented by the venerable Carl Perkins (D), chàirman of the House Education and Labor Committee. Perkins took special interest in the legal battle of one of his constituents, and any education issue would necessarily pass through his committee.

- While the Senate quickly passed Equal Access 88-11, the House twice killed the bill. The day before equal access finally passed on July 25, a federal court of appeals turned thumbs down on the concept but, strangely enough, word of that decision did not reach Washington that day. Nor did it arrive the next day—until ten or fifteen minutes after the close of the 337-77 affirmative vote. The court's action might have turned the House vote around. Why did Congress not know about it in time? I say it respectfully and you can take me literally: God only knows.

- Except for Rep. Perkins, equal access would never have reached the floor of the House that day. Perkins was so incensed by Speaker Tip O'Neill's blatant attempt to bury the bill that he threatened to bypass him with a rare parliamentary procedure, successfully worked just once in the prior quarter century. The Speaker was sufficiently intimidated by Perkins that he capitulated. Equal access got another vote and passed.

That was Carl Perkins' final legislative victory. He was stricken with a fatal heart attack nine days later, on a flight to his beloved old Kentucky home. God preserved his life until well into his seventy-second year. Equal access was his legacy.

The equal access victory teaches us that Christians must do everything humanly possible, while committing the results to God. That's a formula for success in politics— and in all of life.

Anyone claiming that evangelicals won no significant political victories in Washington in the '80s is either igno-rant or bearing false witness. The remarkable thing is that these successes came with the support of only a small per-centage of the evangelical community.

What if hundreds of thousands of other Christians had

joined forces with the comparative handful then involved? What if you, your friends, and your church had been involved? Had that happened, I believe we would have won major, front-page victories in areas such as school prayer or abortion. But we didn't and we haven't—yet.

Notes

1. The four-page *NAE Washington Insight* newsletter is sent to NAE member churches, individuals, or organizations. It is also available by subscription. A special church edition of *Insight* can be ordered in bulk quantities, for distribution in churches and elsewhere. Write for information to the National Association of Evangelicals, Box 28, Wheaton, Illinois 60189. Or, should you prefer, write to NAE Office of Public Affairs, 1023 15th Street, Suite 500, Washington, DC 20005.

2. So troubled was the Evangelical Free Church by the stance of its most prominent layman that it editorialized officially that Anderson was at odds with his own church.

3. Richard A. Viguerie, *The New Right: We're Ready to Lead*, The Viguerie Company, Falls Church, Virginia, 1981, 128.

4. Many of those same evangelicals regard Jimmy Carter as the finest ex-president in their lifetime. They had always respected his personal piety, his persistent witness, and his commitment to the church as manifested in his serving as a regular Sunday school teacher even while president. Today there is more to admire: his refusal to exploit the presidency for personal gain, his servant-role in his work with Habitat for Humanity, and his persistent efforts for peace.

5. From text of Mrs. Reagan's Remarks, 27 July 1988, as released by the White House press office.

6. Ronald Reagan's "Evil Empire" speech is included as Appendix III in this book.

7. Galatians 6:9.

8. 1 Peter 2:13-14.

Steering the Course

Chapter Seven

Are We
"One Nation Under God"?

Although no question mark will be found in his magnificent speech, still, Abraham Lincoln expressed a disquieting uncertainty in his Gettysburg Address: ". . . whether that nation or any nation so conceived and so dedicated can long endure." While his immediate concern was the Civil War, his implicit question is as relevant today as it was on November 19, 1863. The United States of America, as a nation, has no guarantee of perpetuity.

Imagine being included as a participant in a highest-level, off-the-record discussion of the long-range prospects of the United States within the president's National Security Council. Some of the nation's most astute minds would range in two directions, external and internal. Their overarching concern would focus on world peace. While the superpowers have maintained a nuclear stand-off for decades through a policy of Mutual Assured Destruction, what, they would debate, are the possibilities of a world war being triggered by a lesser power through nuclear blackmail? With the Cold War over and the current threat centered in the Arab world's grab for power through control of oil supplies, what potential menaces to peace do they foresee in the next five, ten, or twenty years?

Sooner or later, the president's counselors would turn to the all-important internal issue for the future, the health of the nation's economy. If they were wise, NSC senior staff would do well to call in Treasury's top experts. Discussing whether the free market system will prove adequate for tomorrow's challenges is no topic for international experts alone. It would not be long before the dialogue would turn to topics like the United States' own burgeoning national debt, the inability of many Third World nations to repay their debts, severe problems in America's banking system including the savings and loan industry, trade imbalances, international monetary affairs, and the effects of high taxation.

But if weighty matters such as peace and prosperity comprised the total of that day's conversations, the NSC and their friends from Treasury would have missed the most important issue of all.

A deceptively simple mathematical problem will illustrate my point. Suppose you wish to average sixty miles per hour for a two mile trip. If at the one mile point you have averaged just thirty, how fast must you drive the second mile in order to average sixty?

The obvious answer is ninety, right? Wrong. Sure, 30 + 90 = 120, divided by two yielding an average of sixty, but that answer is incorrect. Ahhh, you say, I get it. If I drive the first mile at half the speed I hope to average, then I must drive the second at double that speed, so the answer is 120. Right? Wrong again.

The fact is that solving our little problem requires inserting into the equation a completely different factor—time. If you average thirty on the first mile, you have already used up two minutes—the total time required to average sixty over two miles. Your hope of averaging sixty is impossible.

In the same way, when the subject is the durability of the United States of America, another completely new factor must be introduced into the equation—not time, but eternity. The NSC folks should have called in a theologian! God Almighty, the maker of heaven and earth, "will judge the world in righteousness."[1] The God before whom "the nations are like a drop in a bucket . . . as dust on the scales"[2] will "judge all the nations on every side."[3] A look at the Old Testament reveals how the Lord of the nations judges nations within history. Even with Israel, there is a cycle: rebellion, retribution, repentance, restoration.

Those who understand and believe biblical teaching know that the God who "sets up kings and deposes them"[4] may one day call down judgment upon our nation. Our national security and longevity are ultimately under his control. For that reason, it is critical to ask: Are we "one nation under God"—as we say we are when we pledge allegiance to the flag?

The average American is far too ignorant of his spiritual heritage. But the fault may lie with others. Textbook writers have cut from the pages of history facts either considered too controversial or unappealing to the educational elites who prefer sanitized books for America's classrooms.

Consider the first half of the Mayflower Compact of 1620, as printed in the Teacher's Guide for the high school history text *Triumph of the American Nation*, published by Harcourt Brace Jovanovich in 1986:

> We whose names are underwritten, having undertaken a voyage to plant the first colony in the northern parts of Virginia, do solemnly and in the presence of God, and one of another, covenant and combine ourselves together into a civil body politic. . . .[5]

Blown off course by storms and arriving in Massachusetts, where their landing is today marked by Plymouth Rock, the Pilgrims came with a much deeper purpose than admitted in that deceptive account, which deletes almost every reference to God. Here, in contrast, is the actual opening of the Mayflower Compact, all words restored (although not in olde English spelling):

> In the name of God, Amen. We whose names are underwritten, the loyal subjects of our dread sovereign lord, King James, by the grace of God, of Great Britain, France, and Ireland, King, Defender of

the Faith, etc., having undertaken for the glory of God and advancement of the Christian faith and honor of our king and country, a voyage to plant the first colony in the northern parts of Virginia, do by these presents solemnly and in the presence of God, and one of another, covenant and combine ourselves together into a civil body politic. . . .

The *vision realized* by our founding fathers—that of "one nation under God"—was a *vision revised* in the mid-twentieth century, and today or tomorrow may well be a *vision revived*.

The Vision Realized

The new nation was conceived with the adoption of the Declaration of Independence on July 4, 1776. The fledgling nation in turn was born with the signing of the Constitution on September 17, 1787. These dates mark the period when our founding fathers realized their vision.

In Deuteronomy, Moses reminded Israel of four historic realities regarding their national relationship to God. I will show that America's founding fathers believed those realities applied to their new nation. Now, I do not suggest there is an exact parallel here. The United States of America is no contemporary equivalent of Israel, God's chosen people of the Old Testament era (and, in the judgment of most evangelicals, a people with whom God still has a special covenant relationship). There is a biblical passage that assuredly does apply to the United States, however. A universal spiritual principle, it pertains to any nation or individual:

From everyone who has been given much, much will be demanded; and from the one who has been entrusted with much, much more will be asked.[6]

Here are the historic realities of God's dealing with Israel as a nation:

• Their *preservation by God*.[7] This had been an enslaved people, led out of oppression and through a terrible wilderness, preserved through miraculous events. While Moses was their leader, he humbly acknowledged that God brought them out.

- The *providence of God*.[8] They would not find their new land through scouting and exploring skills or by chance, but God would bring them to it by his own hand. The land would have an adequate water supply, a good growing climate, and mineral wealth for making agricultural implements.

- Their *prosperity from God*.[9] They would eat well, have time to settle in and build fine homes, and see their flocks and herds reproduce. The land would even include silver and gold for trading and later a monetary system. Beyond all that, God would give them the ability to produce wealth.

- The *punishment of God*.[10] This fact would always be on the horizon, perhaps only as foreboding as a cloud the size of a man's hand, but always there. The people of Israel are clearly told that if they do not honor God, if they flout his will by ignoring or violating his commands, laws, and decrees, then they will be destroyed as a nation. Moses is faithful to declare God's will as straightforwardly as that.

Now let me turn from Israel's sacred text to America's most venerable document, the Declaration of Independence. It is no mere coincidence that the four historic realities recognized by Moses are reflected in the Declaration.

- Their *preservation by God*.

When in the Course of human events, it becomes necessary for one people to dissolve the political bands which have connected them with another, and to assume among the Powers of the earth, the separate and equal station to which the Laws of Nature and of Nature's God entitle them, a decent respect to the opinions of mankind requires that they should declare the causes which impel them to the separation. . . .

The history of the present King of Great Britain is a

history of repeated injuries and usurpations, all having in direct object the establishment of an absolute Tyranny over these States. To prove this, let Facts be submitted to a candid world. . . .

There follows the major body of the Declaration, a list of charges against the king, but the major thrust of these words is that, like Israel, Americans had suffered injustice and tyranny from which they had been preserved. Both natural law and the laws of God in Scripture entitled them to exist separately. As Israel came out of Egypt, our forefathers came out of Europe. Their "wilderness" was a dangerous Atlantic Ocean.

• The *providence of God.*

And for the support of this Declaration, with a firm reliance on the Protection of Divine Providence, we mutually pledge to each other our Lives, our Fortunes, and our sacred Honor.

No explanatory comment is needed about this final sentence of the Declaration, which uses the very theological word in question.

• Their *prosperity from God.*

We hold these truths to be self-evident, that all men are created equal, that they are endowed by their Creator with certain unalienable Rights, that among these are Life, Liberty and the pursuit of Happiness. That to secure these rights, Governments are instituted among Men, deriving their just powers from the consent of the governed. . . .

The founding fathers knew that it would be foolhardy and impossible for government, in and of itself, to provide happiness. However, citizens of this free land would have the right to pursue happiness because of their prior rights to life and liberty—all of which were God-given. That being the case, no government could legitimately claim to grant such rights, but only to guarantee or secure them. Thus, those citizens who pursued financial success in their quest for happiness should literally attribute their prosperity to God.

• The *punishment of God*.

We, therefore, the Representatives of the United States of America, in General Congress, Assembled, appealing to the Supreme Judge of the world for the rectitude of our intentions, do, in the Name, and by authority of the good People of these Colonies, solemnly publish and declare, That these United Colonies are, and of Right ought to be Free and Independent States . . . .

As they separated from the English crown, our forebears called upon God to examine the integrity of their motivation. They tacitly acknowledged that if their intentions were not righteous, they could not expect God's blessing upon their new venture. It is well-nigh impossible to envision a piece of legislation coming from Congress in the 1990s with a respectful call for God to evaluate it. In those days, such words were not surprising.

Can anyone doubt that the authors and signers of the Declaration by common consent acknowledged their political creation to be "one nation under God"? For any skeptics, let us call Thomas Jefferson as a witness. Our third president proposed a national seal portraying Moses leading the chosen people into the promised land, and, in his second inaugural address, in 1805, Jefferson was specific:

. . . I shall need, too, the favor of that Being in whose hands we are, who led our fathers, as Israel of old, from their native land and planted them in a country flowing with all the necessaries and comforts of life; who has covered our infancy with His providence and our riper years with His wisdom and power. . . .

Rep. Guy VanderJagt (R-MI), at the National Prayer Breakfast in February 1980, stated: "Our Declaration of Independence is first of all a declaration of dependence on God." The Founding Fathers would have stood with him. After six months as president, George Washington issued a Proclamation for a National Thanksgiving, including these expressions:

Whereas it is the duty of all nations to acknowledge the providence of Almighty God, to obey His will, to be grateful for His benefits, and humbly to implore His protection and favor. . . . And also that we may then unite in most humbly offering our prayers and supplications to the great Lord and Ruler of Nations, and beseech Him to pardon our national and other transgressions. . . .[11]

Hear part of Washington's first Inaugural Address:

. . . No people can be bound to acknowledge and adore the Invisible Hand which conducts the affairs of men more than those of the United States. . . . We ought to be no less persuaded that the propitious smiles of Heaven can never be expected on a nation that disregards the eternal rules of order and right which Heaven itself has ordained . . . .[12]

Recall Washington's Farewell Address:

Of all the dispositions and habits which lead to political prosperity, Religion and Morality are indispensable supports . . . . Where is the security for property, for reputation, for life, if the sense of religious obligation deserts the oaths which are the instrument of investigation in Courts of Justice? And let us with caution indulge in the supposition that morality can be maintained without religion. Whatever may be conceded to the influence of refined education on minds of peculiar structure, reason and experience both forbid us to expect that national morality can prevail in exclusion of religious principle . . . .[13]

John Adams would become our first vice president and then succeed Washington as our second president. As independence neared, he wrote to his wife Abigail in 1775:

It is Religion and Morality alone which can establish the principles upon which freedom can securely stand. A patriot must be a religious man.[14]

Not long after Washington's inauguration, Adams wrote:

Our Constitution was made only for a moral and religious people. It is wholly inadequate to the government of any other.[15]

Speaking to the first meeting of Congress in Washington, in the original Capitol in 1800, Adams said:

It would be unbecoming the Representatives of this nation to assemble, for the first time, in this solemn temple, without looking up to the Supreme Ruler of the Universe, and imploring his blessing. Here, and throughout our country, may simple manners, pure morals, and true religion, flourish forever![16]

Thomas Jefferson, later to become our third president, in 1781 asked:

Can the liberties of a nation be thought secure when we have removed their only firm basis, a conviction in the minds of the people that these liberties are . . . the gift of God? That they are not to be violated, but with His wrath?[17]

Critics of attempts to demonstrate the biblical beliefs of our founding fathers sometimes dismiss them with a wave: "They weren't really Christians, just a bunch of deists." Through meticulous documentation, John Eidsmoe has demolished the myth that these were mostly secular men in his book, *Christianity and the Constitution—The Faith of Our Founding Fathers.* Reading his in-depth studies of thirteen major founders of our nation, I conclude that in today's terminology eight should be called evangelicals, three would be termed Christians in a broader sense, and only two were deists, Jefferson and Benjamin Franklin. The latter two moved closer to historic Christianity in later years, and some Christian beliefs (of which they might not have been conscious) colored their speech and writings.

Deism is sub-Christian in its "clockmaker" view of the universe, namely, that God created it like a clock already wound up, and then left the world to run down on its own. With that in mind, Jefferson was, at best, an inconsistent deist. His own words, inscribed on the wall of the

Jefferson Memorial, bear witness that he believed in a God of justice who acts in history:

Indeed I tremble for my country when I reflect that God is just: that his justice cannot sleep for ever. . . .

The author of the Bill of Rights, including the First Amendment with its religion clauses, became our fourth president. This was James Madison's conviction:

Before any man can be considered as a member of Civil Society, he must be considered as a subject of the Governor of the Universe.[18]

Except for four vice presidents who came into office on the death of a president and who therefore made no formal inaugural remarks,[19] every president of the United States has sought divine help in his inaugural speech. The tendency today is to downplay such words as a formality, but the kind of strong sentiments uttered by the first four presidents have been sincerely echoed by our most recent presidents, Ronald Reagan and George Bush—and by other twentieth century presidents not of their political ideology.

The fundamental basis of this nation's law was given to Moses on the Mount. The fundamental basis of our Bill of Rights comes from the teachings which we get from Exodus and St. Matthew, from Isaiah and St. Paul. I don't think we emphasize that enough these days. If we don't have the proper fundamental moral background, we will finally wind up with a totalitarian government which does not believe in rights for anybody except the state.

No greater thing could come to our land today than a revival of the spirit of religion—a revival that would sweep through the homes of the nation and stir the hearts of men and women of all faiths to a reassertion of their belief in God and their dedication to His will for themselves and their world. I doubt if there is any problem—social, political or economic—that would not melt away before the fire of such a spiritual awakening.[20]

The first may sound like a quotation from Pat Robertson, but the words were Harry Truman's. The second may resemble comments by Ronald Reagan, but it was Franklin Roosevelt who spoke them.

America's founding fathers did not form a Christian state, but they clearly established their new nation on Judeo-Christian principles found in the Bible.[21] And it's just at this point that I would expect someone to level a charge meant to destroy my case: "God is not even mentioned in the Constitution."

But have these folks actually read the Constitution? After Article VII, I read:

Done in Convention by the Unanimous Consent of the States present the Seventeenth Day of December in the Year of our Lord one thousand seven hundred and eighty seven. . . .

To be technical about it, the name of God is there after all. Let's be fair, however. That was the standard way of signing official documents in those days. Otherwise, God is not mentioned by name. But no matter. The Constitution is the means to secure a specific objective expressed in the Declaration: "That to secure these [God-given] rights, Governments are instituted among Men." The Constitution and its foundational document, the Declaration, cannot be separated.

For the record, John Eidsmoe lists nine cases to buttress his statement that "The Declaration has been repeatedly cited by the U.S. Supreme Court as part of the fundamental law of the United States of America."[22]

The Vision Revised

A 1947 decision appeared to provide the Supreme Court an opportunity to "baptize" into the Constitution a phrase that had never been there—and in so doing, to revise our forefathers' vision of "one nation under God." It is not necessary to know the details of *Everson v. Board of Education*, but rather to learn that, in *Everson*, the court for the first time said that the Non-establishment clause of the First Amendment "was intended to erect 'a wall of separation between church and state.'" Enlarging on the concept, Justice Black wrote: "That wall must be kept high and impregnable."

Everson became the pivotal case for establishment issues, for four decades influencing the court's decisions in a direction not in accord with historic facts. While the pendulum has begun to swing back in recent years, the interpretation and imagery of a high and impregnable wall of separation has guided the court toward secularizing the United States, often creating an impression of hostility toward religion.

Seven years later, however, Congress appeared to challenge this view of separation when it added to the words of the pledge of allegiance the phrase "under God." What possible secular purpose could that 1954 action have had? The Congress compounded its challenge when it ordered the inscription "In God We Trust" to be placed on our money, and when it made the phrase our national motto—an admission that the state is not sovereign unto itself, but accountable to a higher authority.

Was court or Congress correct? The historical documents and facts do not lead to the conclusion that the framers of the First Amendment and the Congress responsible for its adoption into the Constitution intended a wall of absolute separation between church and state. However—and this is a critical point—there are those who contend that what the framers intended is oftentimes impossible to determine, and in any case not binding for today. Some of them are Supreme Court justices.

The 1983 case of *Marsh v. Chambers* illustrates the issue. The High Court considered the constitutionality of Nebraska's paying a minister to serve as chaplain to its legislature, to open each session with prayer. Happily, by a six-to-three vote the court approved the practice. In the majority opinion, Chief Justice Burger pointed out that the first Congress authorized the appointment of paid chaplains for both the Senate and House just three days before it reached final agreement on the language of the Bill of Rights. "Clearly the men who wrote the First Amendment Religion Clause did not view paid legislative chaplains and opening prayers as a violation of that Amendment," he wrote. Incidentally, James Madison, author of the First Amendment, served on the congressional committee of six that recommended the chaplain system.

As important as was the affirmation in *Marsh*, the three dissenting votes are extremely significant. In this case, all the justices had been made aware of the historical sequence above, so that it was not necessary to engage in conjecture about the intent of the founders. Nonetheless, three justices were willing to say, in effect, that paid chaplains in state legislatures should be held unconstitutional. To them, what the framers intended was beside the point. They were willing to substitute their personal predilection for a strict interpretation of the Constitution—an act of judicial activism.

Renowned constitutional attorney William Bentley Ball candidly condemns the activist approach by which judges seek to correct what they see as abuses in the system, which legislative bodies have failed to remedy. Said Ball: "The Constitution must govern our judges, and not the reverse." Judges who share that attitude bring judicial restraint to the bench, seeing their job only as interpreting the Constitution. Think of the consequences if the Supreme Court should have a majority of activists. Unanchored as they would be, five non-elected justices, serving for life, could create a sociological revolution in American society. Some would say the court already has.

To grasp once and for all the importance of judicial philosophy, think of an analogy: What the Bible is to Christianity, the Constitution is to the United States—in both cases the absolute, final, written authority. If you take a liberal view of the Bible, by which the words are not necessarily binding and the intent of the author is irrelevant, then the form of Christianity that you develop may bear little resemblance to the intent of the Founding Father in heaven. By the same token, if you take a liberal view of the Constitution, the nation that you shape may not resemble the intent of America's founding fathers. In that light, anyone can see how it has been possible for the court to revise the founders' original vision. The original intent of the framers must be determined whenever it can be. Further, we must realize the great importance of selecting presidents, because they appoint judges.

One loose end remains. Where did the "wall of separation" concept originate, and how did it play out in the originator's life? In 1802, President Thomas Jefferson interpreted his understanding of the First Amendment to the Danbury Baptist Association of Connecticut. He was writing eleven years after the First Amendment was approved, and not as a jurist. While he probably was not suggesting that religion be walled off, his terminology caught on and came to be accepted as what the Constitution implied.

Now for the second part of the question. How did Jefferson apply his own concept of the "wall"? In 1803, a year after the Danbury letter, President Jefferson made a treaty with the Kaskaskia Indians in which he pledged federal money to support their priest and to build them a Catholic church.[23] Later that year he sought funds from Congress to finance the obligations of the treaty. It is more than mildly astounding that the author of the "wall of separation" concept asked Congress to fund religious activity in his own time. It is, therefore, unthinkable that Jefferson would have allowed his country to be sanitized of religiously-based values so that it could no longer be considered "under God."

The Vision Revived

In the opinion of some thoughtful political analysts, a movement to revive the "one nation under God" vision of the founding fathers began to develop in the last decade. "Forget nuclear freezes and yuppies," wrote *New Republic* senior editor Fred Barnes. "The most important political development of the '80s is the emergence of the evangelical voting bloc."[24]

Millions of evangelicals might not have been able to analyze the reasons for their unprecedented involvement in politics, but they were responding either to the calls of respected Christian leaders or to a growing uneasiness in their own minds. The nation's moral codes were being revised, aided and abetted by the courts and the Congress. Government agencies seemed to be getting their noses under the tent of the churches' religious liberty.

Moreover, the bottom line for evangelicals' burgeoning political interest is the conviction that God's commands are for our good. Individually, those who violate God's laws are sure to be hurt. That is true of both spiritual and physical laws. Try defying the law of centrifugal force by turning into your driveway while tooling along at fifty miles per hour. If you don't overturn your car, you must live on an estate with a long entry road. Nationally, when a nation flouts God's moral and spiritual principles, it is in for tough times. One Old Testament chapter devotes sixty-eight verses to the blessings of national obedience and the curses of national disobedience.[25]

Even if some of their fellow citizens do not appreciate it, evangelicals are now self-consciously serving their culture by devoting themselves to political values consistent with their understanding of the Bible. They are eager to see their nation willingly acknowledge itself to be "one nation under God." Having read some of the founders' convictions earlier in this chapter, they will be delighted to find themselves in such distinguished company as the first presidents.

What is more, evangelicals are strengthening our national foundations from a sociological standpoint as well as a spiritual one. In an article on "Democracy and Religion," the Brookings Institution's James Reichley explored the relation between democratic and Judeo-Christian values.[26] He took issue with many of his peers:

The Founders, who included among their number some of the most acute political theorists the nation ever produced, did not share the disinterest in religion of more recent generations of political scientists. Apparently they knew something today's academics have missed. Reichley summarizes the secular sources which can be expected to support democratic institutions. He finds three:

[1] Social habit, conveyed through custom and tradition. . . . But habit separated from belief in the objective reality of the assumptions out of which habit grows will eventually run dry.

Since the Enlightenment, social and political theorists who distrusted religion, or regarded it as unbelievable, have tried to develop secular philosophies that would give democratic societies enough cohesion to function, while at the same time preserving moral imperatives upholding freedom and equality. This effort has proceeded along two main tracks. Some social philosophers, mostly British and American, have built on the tradition, originated by Thomas Hobbes and John Locke in the seventeenth century, of deriving all social values from [2] rational pursuit of individual self-interest . . . . Others, mostly central European, following routes blazed by Rousseau, Kant, Hegel, and Marx, have produced doctrines offering personal emancipation through [3] submergence of the individual in an idealized general will. . . .

History teaches that there are serious flaws in these philosophies. Reichley can only conclude that

. . . the Founders' conviction that republican government needs the guidance and support of religious principles remains persuasive . . . . Democracy, for its part, depends, now and for the foreseeable future, on values that have no reliable source outside religion.

The conclusion of Will and Ariel Durant, in their monumental *Story of Civilization*, is similar to Reichley's. They assert that, without a standard of public morality, no society has survived. Corollary to that, no moral standard has survived without a religious sanction.

Evangelicals have cause to be deeply concerned about Lincoln's haunting question, "whether that nation or any nation so conceived or so dedicated can long endure." If they and many of their fellow Americans cannot revive the vision of the founders, their nation will be in jeopardy. Given the loss of our moral consensus and the serious deterioration of our culture in the United States today, it is tragically evident that we are not "one nation under God." But we could be.

Notes

1. Psalm 96:13; 98:9.

2. Isaiah 40:15.

3. Joel 3:12.

4. Daniel 2:21.

5. *Education Update*, Heritage Foundation, Vol. 10, No. 3, Summer 1987.

6. Luke 12:48.

7. Deuteronomy 8:1-5, 14b-16.

8. Deuteronomy 8:7-9.

9. Deuteronomy 8:10-13, 18.

10. Deuteronomy 8:1, 6, 11, 17-20.

11. Robert L. Cord, *Separation of Church and State: Historical Fact and Current Fiction* (New York: Lambeth Press, 1982), 51f.

12. Benjamin Weiss, *God in American History* (Grand Rapids: Zondervan, 1966), 51f.

13. John Eidsmoe, *Christianity and the Constitution* (Grand Rapids: Baker Book House, 1987), 119.

14. A. James Reichley, *Religion in American Public Life* (Washington, D.C.: The Brookings Institution, 1985), 104.

15. Ibid., 105.

16. *Congressional Record*, 18 July 1990, S 9885.

17. Eidsmoe, 227.

18. Eidsmoe, 88.

19. John Tyler, Millard Fillmore, Andrew Johnson, and Chester Arthur.

20. Bob Arnebeck, "FDR Invoked God, Too," *Washington Post*, 21 September 1986.

21. I am well aware of the scholarly debate, even among evangelicals, over the nature of America's spiritual heritage. In their book, *The Search for Christian America*, authors Mark Noll, Nathan Hatch, and George Marsden argue that early America does not deserve to be called Christian, and that such an idea is at best an ambiguous concept. On the other hand, in his *Defending the Declaration*, Gary Amos is "horrified" at the conclusions in Noll, Hatch, and Marsden's book.

22. Eidsmoe, 360.

23. President Washington made a similar treaty with the Oneida, Tuscarora, and Stockbridge Indians in January 1795.

24. Barnes frequently appears on network public affairs television shows. He had a privileged hour in the sun during the first Reagan-Mondale television debate of the '84 campaign. As a member of the panel of questioners, he asked whether either candidate was a born-again Christian. Fred had recently come to Christian faith at that time, and was not trying to throw the candidates a curve, but to elicit a positive confession of faith if that were possible. Both Reagan and Mondale managed to dodge the question.

25. Deuteronomy 28.

26. *PS*, a publication of the American Political Science Association, Fall 1986, 801-806.

Chapter Eight

Who Will Determine America's Future?

When the founding fathers met in their 1787 Constitutional Convention, they quickly determined that the Articles of Confederation under which they had been operating were inadequate for a national government. As they set out to "invent" a new nation, they agreed to do so in utmost secrecy. George Washington one day scolded the delegates when a written resolution was found on the floor: "I must entreat, gentlemen, to be more careful lest our transactions get into the News Papers and disturb the public repose by premature speculations."

Given today's poking and prying media, electronic transmission of news, and politicians willing to leak inside information, it seems incredible that when the convention was over, an old lady could accost Benjamin Franklin just outside the doors of Philadelphia's Constitution Hall and ask: "Well, Dr. Franklin, what have we got, a Republic or a Monarchy?" Franklin's reply was classic: "A Republic, Madam, if you can keep it."[1]

For more than two hundred years we have maintained our Republic, even through difficult times of testing like a Civil War, two World Wars, the Great Depression following the stock market crash of 1929, and a fiercely unpopular war in Vietnam. Now, early in the 1990s, the United States of America confronts as severe a test as the nation has ever faced—although some Americans scoff at such an assertion and express pleasure at the direction our culture is moving. That doesn't surprise me. It has always been true that "There is a way that seems right to a man, but in the end it leads to death."[2]

Our nation's cultural drift has brought us to a cultural crisis serious enough to be called a "culture war." If it is true that God Almighty is the ultimate umpire over the nations, then losing that war of values could find us rereading *The Decline and Fall of the Roman Empire* in an attempt to discover where we went wrong. We are engaged in a culture war for the soul of America.

Just a glance at the title of Charles Colson's *Against the Night: Living in the New Dark Ages* tells a great deal. Colson senses that a "crisis of immense proportion is upon us," and begins by mentioning others with similar forebodings.

Carl Henry writes of the twilight of our culture; Malcolm Muggeridge predicts the end of Christendom. Francis Schaeffer warns of the spiritual collapse of the West. Even secular journals sound the alarm. *Newsweek* declares "the American century . . . over," and *Time* decries a "moral malaise overhanging American life."

. . . the crisis that threatens us, the force that could topple our monuments and destroy our very foundations, is within ourselves. The crisis is in the character of our culture, where the values that restrain inner vices and develop inner virtues are eroding. Unprincipled men and women, disdainful of their moral heritage and skeptical of Truth itself, are destroying our civilization by weakening the very pillars upon which it rests.[3]

In an address to the 1990 convention of National Religious Broadcasters, psychologist James Dobson said that "We are engaged at this time in an enormous civil war of values." He portrayed Judeo-Christian values at loggerheads with a humanistic, avant-garde perspective that recognizes no absolute values, adding: "What most people don't realize is that our children are the prize. Those who control what children see, hear, and are taught control the nation." A *New York Times* feature on Dobson and his Focus on the Family ministry reported:

. . . an average of ten thousand often heart-wrenching letters a month [are sent to Focus on the Family].

"Through this department we are watching the unraveling of a social order," Mr. Dobson said. "Five years ago people wrote us about thumb-sucking and bed-wetting. Now they're writing about wife beating, child abuse, manic depression, suicide, and satanic cults."

Mr. Dobson has been worrying about the unraveling of the social order since the 1960s, when he said he was appalled by what he viewed as the impact of sexual and cultural permissiveness on people he was treating in family counseling.

America's and evangelicals' leading theologian, Carl F.H. Henry, has spoken with prophetic wisdom for decades. From the long perspective of history he wrote *Twilight of a Great Civilization* in 1988.

Never has the need for a culture enlivened by the moral law of God been more urgent than in our generation when social tumult obscures the very patterns of normalcy, and in fact increasingly champions the normless. In a culture dominated by a neo-pagan mind and will, deviation tends to become the norm, and normalcy in turn is perversely declared deviant. That cultural condition is the midnight hour for an evangelical alternative that seeks to count for something significant before the collapse and ruination of the contemporary social scene.[4]

On Capitol Hill, Rep. Henry Hyde (R-IL) is one of Congress's most effective debaters and a champion of the right to life. He is known for his commitment to traditional moral values.

. . . the Great Arts Controversy demonstrated that America is, in truth, involved in a Kulturkampf—a culture war, a war between cultures and a war about the very meaning of "culture."

It is best to be precise about the terminology here. By "culture war," I don't mean arguments over the relative merits of Mozart and Beethoven. . . . Nor do I mean the tensions between highbrows and low-brows, between sports fans and opera buffs, between people who think Bruce Springsteen is the greatest artist alive and people who wouldn't know Bruce Springsteen if he rang their doorbell and asked to use the telephone.

No, by "culture war" I mean the struggle between those who believe that the norms of "bourgeois morality" (which is drawn in the main from classic Jewish and Christian morality) should form the ethical basis of our common life, and those who are determined that those norms will be replaced with a radical and thoroughgoing moral relativism. That the "relativism" in question is as absolutist and as condescendingly self-righteous as any sixteenth-century inquisitor is a nice irony. But that is the division in our house.[5]

Conservative columnist Patrick J. Buchanan in a March 26, 1990 column wrote of the root of the arts community's battle to secure unrestricted federal grants:

The arts crowd is after more than our money, more than an end to the congressional ban on funding obscene and blasphemous art. It is engaged in a cultural struggle to root out the old America of family, faith, and flag, and recreate society in a pagan image.

The maneuvering in America's Kulturkampf is over, the forces are now engaged; and, a bewildered and defensive Christian society is absorbing one blow after another.

. . . This is a war about the fundamental values of the country . . . the battle for America's soul.

The idea that we are now absorbed in a civil war over cultural values is not contrived by paranoid religionists. One among numerous such references, the *Washington Post* recently emblazoned the front page of its "Show" section with the headline: "Who's Winning the Culture Wars?"[6]

Living in exile in the United States, one of the most courageous and perceptive men of our century thinks that the wrong forces are winning. In a *Time* interview, Aleksandr Solzhenitsyn hit the nail on the head in responding to a question about the decline of the West's moral life:

> There is technical progress, but this is not the same thing as the progress of humanity as such. In every civilization this process is very complex. In Western Civilizations—which used to be called Western-Christian but now might better be called Western-Pagan—along with the development of intellectual life and science, there has been a loss of the serious moral basis of society.[7]

It is important that no one think that by "culture" we mean preferences, tastes, and manners—in the context of our nation, or any nation for that matter.

> What is culture? It is the ways of thinking, living, and behaving that define a people and underlie its achievements. It is a nation's collective mind, its sense of right and wrong, the way it perceives reality, and its definition of self. Culture is the morals and habits a mother strives to instill in her children. It is the obligations we acknowledge toward our neighbors, our community, and our government. It is the worker's dedication to craftsmanship and the owner's acceptance of the responsibilities of stewardship. It is the standards we set and enforce for ourselves and for others: our definitions of duty, honor, and character. It is our collective conscience.[8]

By that or any other realistic definition of culture, our nation is sliding down a slippery slope toward decadence, gathering speed as it goes. Whether evangelicals will now seize the opportunity to steer America's course—something potentially within their grasp—remains to be seen. That possibility is the reason for this book.

Before the final challenge, let's look at the competing philosophies behind this civil war within our culture. Reduced to bare bones, the battle is between cultural conservatism and cultural radicalism. The conservative approach ascribes great value to the accumulated wisdom of the culture, and considers disciplined behavior most likely to bring happiness in the long run. The radical approach gives great worth to novelty and diversity, and tends to find its satisfaction in immediate gratification.

The founding fathers assuredly would have taken sides with cultural conservatism, for they often insisted that Christianity and government must work together "to raise the virtue and morality of the people to a level at which they are sufficiently public-spirited and self-restrained that republican government can work."[9]

This distinction becomes more pointed when one realizes that the ethical standard of Western civilization was the Bible. Cultural radicals are often in direct rebellion against those Judeo-Christian values, unwilling to discipline themselves by any standard beyond themselves. The founders made social compacts or covenants with each other, God being their witness, and those commitments were a sufficient glue to hold their nation together. By contrast, cultural radicals abhor moral limitations, that is, religiously based values, and exalt the quest for individual rights as their greatest good. But 250 million people pursuing their own rights simply will not produce a glue that can hold their society together.

In a speech addressed to a small group of political strategists, conservative political thinker Paul Weyrich developed the case for cultural conservatism:

> Democracy is the one form of government which depends for its success and existence upon a virtuous

people. Democracy works only so long as a sufficient proportion of the people are willing to place the common good above self-interest, and only so long as there is a broad consensus on what constitutes value.[10]

Once again, Aleksandr Solzhenitsyn touches the sore spot of excessive individualism:

... we have two lungs. You can't breathe with just one lung and not with the other. We must avail ourselves of rights and duties in equal measure. And if this is not established by the law, if the law does not oblige us to do that, then we have to control ourselves. When Western society was established, it was based on the idea that each individual limited his own behavior. Everyone understood what he could do and what he could not do. The law itself did not restrain people. Since then, the only thing we have been developing is rights, rights, rights, at the expense of duty.[11]

America's younger generation is conditioned toward cultural radicalism today by public education. Allan Bloom's book, *The Closing of the American Mind*, to widespread astonishment established itself on national best-seller lists in mid-1987. This was neither a fluke nor a public relations triumph, but testimony to the force of Bloom's message. The University of Chicago professor attacked liberalism for selling collegians a bill of goods, namely, that there is no standard for distinguishing between right and wrong, or good and bad:

... today's university student believes one thing deeply. It has reached the status of an axiom. He is absolutely convinced that truth is relative, and he is astonished if anyone is foolish enough to challenge the point.

This relativism is not the product of theoretical reasoning. It is, so the student believes, a moral postulate of a free society. He has been taught from childhood that the danger of absolutism is not error but intolerance. Thus in our democratic society, says Bloom, openness is the highest virtue . . . the supreme insight is not to think you are right at all.[12]

The other side of the coin of tolerance is to repudiate the conclusions of "true believers" of any sort—including evangelicals with their belief in revealed truth and moral absolutes. No wonder evangelicals are called narrow-minded, religious zealots, bigoted fundamentalists, censors, or anti-choice activists. And all of that just for failing to smile upon promiscuity, drugs, euthanasia, homosexual lifestyles, or taking the life of a unborn child for convenience—at the same time trying to get government not to condone such practices.

Popular campus speaker Josh McDowell says that in the 1940s, "the three most common [school] disciplinary problems were talking, chewing gum, and running in the halls. In the 1980s the statistics say the most common problems are rape, robbery, and assault."[13] Our society is paying the price of the sexual revolution, enhanced by values-clarification teaching techniques that undermine values transmitted by home and church, along with the refusal of teachers to take moral positions. A recent cartoon spoofed this educational craziness under the title, "If drug education were taught like sex education." In the cartoon's four frames, the teacher speaks to the children seated before her:

I would like to encourage all of you not to use drugs at all. But since this is a public school and I'm not allowed to inflict my own puritan beliefs on you . . . and since I know that many of you will be active with drugs from time to time, today's class will be on how to practice safe drug use. . . . This is a hypodermic syringe. You should use this if you want to inject drugs directly into your veins. Notice how it is sealed so the user can tell the needle is clean. . . . It's important you use clean needles when you inject drugs into your body. If you don't have clean needles, check with the school nurse and she will give you some. Now, let me show you how to find the vein.

Since many traditional values are no longer being conserved through public education, and because all that remains to be taught is a value-system of secular humanism, society is terribly weakened—the consequences seen in multitudes of individual students pursuing intense sexual experiences, drug episodes, and materialism. Worst of all, many will hear their parents' "dogmatic religion" mocked, and parental authority undercut.

By far the greatest cost of cultural radicalism can be found in damaged families. Society's acceptance of relativism and individualism, portrayed and subtly advanced through much of television's banal programming, has led to practices that can demolish the marriage bond: use of pornography, permissive sex, and easy divorce. What will it take to restore the life-long, faithful marriage of a man and woman as America's most honored lifestyle? What will it take to restore respect for parental values so that children will ignore the siren lure of heavy metal or rap music which centers on satanism, suicide, deviant sex, drug usage, or sadomasochism?

Some years ago, I recall D. James Kennedy suggesting that in our nation the cold air mass of unbelief had collided with the warm air mass of Christianity, to produce a severe storm front. One system of thought begins with God, the other in unaided human wisdom, assuming that it will be able to discover everything it needs to know in time—that is, before death. The apostle Paul contrasts those views:

> Where is the wise man? Where is the scholar? Where is the philosopher of this age? Has not God made foolish the wisdom of the world? For since in the wisdom of God the world through its wisdom did not know him, God was pleased through the foolishness of what was preached to save those who believe.

> We do, however, speak a message of wisdom among the mature, but not the wisdom of this age or of the rulers of this age, who are coming to nothing. No, we speak of God's secret wisdom, a wisdom that has been hidden and that God destined for our glory before time began. None of the rulers of this age

understood it, for if they had, they would not have crucified the Lord of glory.[14]

Insofar as thought leaders continue to rebel against the Judeo-Christian principles commonly accepted by the founders, our nation is in increasing peril. As much as evangelicals deplore the cultural crisis, they do discern its source:

> For our struggle is not against flesh and blood, but against the rulers, against the authorities, against the powers of this dark world . . .[15]

To see the progress of the culture war, let's look at several fronts where cultural radicalism is attacking cultural conservatism today. Battles are being fought over radical feminism, abortion rights, arts funding, and homosexual rights.

• *Radical Feminism* must be distinguished from feminism spelled with a lower case f. I applaud the many breakthroughs women have achieved in our time which give them equal dignity and opportunity with men. Legitimate feminism squares with the biblical assurance of equal worth before God:

> There is neither Jew nor Greek, slave nor free, male nor female, for you are all one in Christ Jesus.[16]

On the other hand, when one understands the implications of the "patriarchal oppression" claimed by many feminists, one realizes that radical feminism bluntly rejects the will of the Creator who made male and female, and who stipulated the nature of the marriage relationship.

> The bottom line of the Feminist agenda is this: For women to be liberated they must be relieved of the responsibility of childcare; the nuclear family must metamorphose.[17]

Beyond insisting that the sex/gender system is of crucial importance, and that women must break away from male domination by controlling their own reproduction and work role, radical feminism is capsuled in the hateful aphorism, "A woman needs a man like a fish needs a bicycle." In feminist literature one finds suggestions for abolishing marriage, preferring bisexuality or androgyny, and hoping for the day when science will make it possible for women to impregnate one another.[18]

Such thinking runs in many perverse directions. In 1983, the New York City Council passed an ordinance requiring public places selling alcoholic beverages to post warnings that drinking while pregnant can cause birth defects. The president of the New York chapter of the National Organization for Women shocked Mayor Ed Koch by her letter urging him to veto the ordinance. She complained of "discrimination" in singling out pregnant women as a class, and then objected to "protecting the unborn at the expense of women's freedom."[19] NOW's national office refused to verify or deny that the morally bankrupt reasoning of that New York letter represented the organization's official position.

Radical feminism positions itself in opposition to Judeo-Christian principles. Tragically, with the aid of the media, some of our daughters and granddaughters are being radicalized, to their personal detriment and that of their family and nation.

• The battle over *Abortion Rights* involves "the greatest civil rights issue of our time and defines our national character," according to Catholic lay theologian George Weigel.[20] It is shocking to realize how far our nation has drifted from its historic respect for the God-given right to life. According to Harvard Professor of Law Mary Ann Glendon, to find a nation "as indifferent to unborn life" as the United States, it is necessary to look beyond the West, beyond Europe, and even beyond the Soviet bloc. Only in nations such as China, where concerns about economics and population growth supersede all else, will an equally disdainful attitude toward life be found.

Paul Weyrich places this into the context of our cultural clash:

> Defense of the right to life responds to such basic American values as compassion for the weak, equality of rights, and reverence for life . . . .

Abortion is not an issue in a vacuum. It is the symbol for a cultural cleavage between those with a sense of community and responsibility and the votaries of imperial individualism; between . . . those who worship in churches and those who mock religion; those who accept our culture and those who seek to tear it down.[21]

Charles Colson quotes Pat Buchanan as underlining America's lack of a moral consensus:

Americans of left and right no longer share the same religion, the same values, the same codes of morality; we only inhabit the same piece of land.

The cultural radicals have been winning the popular battle over abortion, although there is hope that the Supreme Court may before long reverse the infamous 1973 *Roe v. Wade* decision that opened the door to abortion on demand. Pro-abortion rights forces have succeeded, with the all-too-willing connivance of the media,[22] in couching the issue in terms either for or against the right of choice—never mind the nature of the choice, the snuffing out of an unborn child's life. Being anti-choice, in and of itself, is neither good or bad. It would be admirable in many situations. Would anyone argue that Americans should be pro-choice on slavery, burglary, or racial discrimination?

• *Government funding of the arts* provided a fierce firefight at the turn of the decade from '89 to '90. The battle erupted over the so-called "art" of Andres Serrano, featuring a photograph of a crucifix submerged in a jar of the artist's own urine. What made the matter incredible was that Serrano's work was funded by taxpayers' dollars through a grant from the National Endowment for the Arts.

That was just the beginning. Over the next months, we would discover that the NEA had funded live sex act performances, homoerotic displays, and other sacrilegious and salacious "art." The arts community resisted any restrictions whatever on its creativity, charging cultural conservatives with attempts to censor creativity. The arts elite steadfastly refused to concede that sponsorship was the issue, not censorship. One columnist imagined the liberal elite boasting, "You pathetic peasants. We're not only going to produce works which offend your deepest sensibilities, but we'll force you to pay for them as well."

As painful as it is to admit it, Ken Myers is probably correct. The cultural chasm in America today may be so wide that cultural radicals cannot comprehend why pornographic or blasphemous art is so troublesome to cultural conservatives.

> If Jesse Helms and Don Wildmon were shocked on first seeing "Piss Christ," the arts community, which takes such work for granted, was just as shocked that anyone minded, like perplexed cannibals wondering why the missionaries want to tamper with their menu.[23]

• Finally, *Homosexual Rights* may provoke the bitterest and most prolonged battle of all. Homosexuals seem determined to make this decade "The Gay Nineties" in a manner unthinkable a century ago. Their agenda? Jeffrey Levi, of the National Gay and Lesbian Task Force, was frank in his address to the National Press Club on October 9, 1987. He spoke of demanding passage of a federal gay and lesbian civil rights bill:

> But our agenda is becoming broader than that; we are no longer seeking just a right to privacy and a right to protection from wrong. We also have a right—as heterosexual Americans have already—to see government and society affirm our lives. Now that is a statement that may make some of our liberal friends queasy. But the truth is, until our relationships are recognized in the law—through domestic partner legislation or the definition of beneficiary, for example—until we are provided the same financial incentives in tax law and government programs to encourage our family relationships, then we will not have achieved equality in American society.[24]

Gary Bauer, president of the Family Research Council, summarized the threat to society. The pattern?

The abnormal seeks tolerance, then demands acceptance, and, finally, argues for government subsidies and the granting of special rights.[25]

If the current situation doesn't remind you of Isaiah's prophecy, it should:

Woe to those who call evil good
    and good evil,
who put darkness for light
    and light for darkness,
who put bitter for sweet
    and sweet for bitter. . . .
Therefore, as tongues of fire lick up straw
    and as dry grass sinks down in the flames,
so their roots will decay
    and their flowers blow away like dust;
for they have rejected the law of the
    LORD Almighty
and spurned the word of the
    Holy One of Israel.[26]

Homosexuals have made significant gains in recent years. They have managed to make AIDS a politically protected disease, giving it more of a civil rights emphasis than that of a public health issue. They have thrown some denominations into turmoil by demanding ordination to the ministry. In 1988, they secured the support of all the potential Democratic presidential nominees. In 1990, to their great surprise, several gay activists were invited to the White House for bill-signing ceremonies. But the most significant part of their battle in the culture war was fought in the District of Columbia.

In 1988, homosexuals employed a D.C. human rights statute to force Roman Catholic Georgetown University to grant space and funds to a gay rights group on campus. After a two-year effort, thanks to the leadership of Sen. Bill Armstrong, Congress acted through the appropriations bill to allow church-affiliated schools to decide for themselves whether they would give money or recognition to groups promoting or condoning homosexuality. Twice during the battle NAE pulled together a press conference, with a broad supporting coalition, to urge passage of the Armstrong amendment and to clarify that this was a religious liberty issue, not gay-bashing as alleged.

Our press conference statement suggested that requiring Georgetown to fund gay rights advocates made as much sense as compelling Hebrew Union College to fund a campus chapter of a neo-Nazi group, or black Howard University to support a chapter of the Ku Klux Klan.

No conflict better illustrates the clash between cultural conservatives and cultural radicals. Stripped of all emotion and posturing, the issue was this: Can religious schools be forced to subsidize groups promoting beliefs and practices contrary to the schools' religious beliefs? The Roman Catholic university believes homosexual behavior to be sin. Sad to say, although cultural conservatives won this time, about one-third of the senators and representatives showed by their votes that they preferred gay rights over religious freedom. Can we allow their kind of thinking to become the majority mindset in the Congress of the United States?

Pressure for gay rights never seems to let up. Senator Armstrong again had to do battle in the summer of 1990. The D.C. government required organizations like Big Brothers and Girl Scouts to admit homosexuals into their ranks as counselors, coaches, and leaders. Armstrong finally prevailed, after losing the first time around, as the Senate by 54-45 decided on September 12 that such organizations should have the right to exclude homosexuals as role models, if they wished to do so. The frightening aspect of the vote is that a minority of forty-five believe the District of Columbia should be allowed to force youth organizations to include homosexuals in their leadership.

In the civil war of the '90s, government must uphold conservative cultural values if our society is to endure.

Unfortunately, government's resolve is weakening. Cultural radicals are winning many battles on the major fronts described above—although not on all fronts, by any means.

The question at the beginning of this chapter demands an answer: Who will determine America's future? Who will win the coming civil war?

Ronald Reagan was fond of saying, "The greatest revolution in history began with the words, 'We the people.'" I believe the greatest revival of a nation in history must begin with the words, "We the evangelicals."

To bring spiritual revival to the United States will require the commitment of millions of Christians who take the Bible seriously. To bring political renewal to that nation will require those same people. One of the Scripture's most significant texts ties the two together:

> If my people, who are called by my name, will humble themselves and pray and seek my face and turn from their wicked ways, then will I hear from heaven and will forgive their sin and will heal their land.[27]

Spiritual and political renewal will not come when only the three conditions of personal piety are met. There is a fourth condition, involving repentance and changed lives, an abrupt swing away from sinful ways. As evangelicals, our most common political sin is not one of commission, but of omission—remaining aloof from politics, uncaring about the culture war, selfishly tending our own homestead. When we reject our own ignorance and apathy and start actively working for righteousness in politics and government, then, just then, God may act to heal our land. And in years when political leaders struggle with "the vision thing," who but the church can offer a moral vision to society?

This is the time for evangelicals to grab history's helm and to determine America's course. When they do, they should not be surprised to find millions of cultural conservatives—whether they would call themselves that or not—willing to follow. Evangelicals have sufficient *reason,* adequate *resources*, and every *right* to attempt to take the political lead.

Evangelicals have multiple reasons to engage in the political life of the nation in an unprecedented way. They are beginning to understand the current crisis, they know that God is honored when they work for righteousness in society, and they have every reason to believe that God can multiply their efforts just as surely as Jesus multiplied a boy's bread and fish to feed five thousand.

Not long after he had been released from prison for a Watergate-related offense, Charles Colson chanced upon an interview with Carl Henry in the *Washington Star*. The words, he testifies today, hit him powerfully and deeply affected his understanding of the "continuing conflict between our Christian values and modern culture. . . ." This was the heart of the interview:

> The intellectual decision most urgently facing humanity in our time is whether to acknowledge or disown Jesus Christ as the hope of the world and whether Christian values are to be the arbiter of human civilization in the present instead of only in the final judgment of men and nations.[28]

Evangelicals clearly have the material resources to exert a decisive influence upon this nation. To counter cultural radicalism, there are more than 1,100 Christian radio stations and over 350 Christian television stations in the country. Thirty million people, according to researcher George Barna, read Christian magazines regularly. Over $30 billion is donated to Christian churches every year, with $8 to 10 billion more given to parachurch ministries.[29]

More Americans attend church or synagogue on any one weekend, four of ten,[30] than attend all professional football, baseball, and basketball games in an entire year. George Gallup asserts that "America is unique in the world for the high levels of religious belief among its educated people." His mid-1990 research shows that 38 percent of Americans describe themselves as evangelicals, or born-again

Christians, while his annual report shows 33 percent. Gallup explains that some people may be hesitant to use those terms of themselves, but that "alternatively worded questions have yielded similar results." High percentages hold conservative theological views, for example, regarding the deity of Christ or his resurrection from the dead.

At the same time, almost half of Americans (48 percent) see religion as losing influence in society. With the right kind of leadership, many could be mobilized. Even allowing for exaggerations in the numbers—although Gallup's reputation as a pollster is impeccable—evangelicals have the potential political resources to change the nation.

They also have the spiritual resources. Their confidence in the sovereignty of God was reaffirmed by the crumbling of communism in Eastern Europe in 1989. They believe, with many of Israel's kings in the Old Testament, that "the battle is the Lord's."[31]

Happily for them, evangelicals have the right to advance their convictions in the public square. They have not been gerrymandered out of the political arena because they bring religious beliefs into the battle. Under the Constitution, they have full freedom to use their citizenship rights. Evangelicals are likely to recall a vivid biblical image: "See, I have placed before you an open door that no one can shut."[32]

The door may be open at just the right time. Declining voter turnout over the last two decades plays into the hands of evangelicals, provided they can mobilize their constituency better than others. After all, the value of a vote is relative to the total number of votes cast. To illustrate, 24,000 voted in my 1976 primary election in Colorado, while 240,000 voted in November. A vote in September thus had ten times the clout of a vote that November. Further, America has never had as high a percentage of older people as it has today. Those people are most likely to have conservative cultural values, and they go to the polls in greater numbers than any other age group. On the other hand, the eighteen to twenty-four generation "knows less, cares less, and reads newspapers less" than any generation in the last fifty years.[33] Especially vulnerable to the individualistic, relativistic, and hedonistic spirit of the times, it is fortunate that, unlike their elders, they send a low percentage of their number to the polls.

In spite of my optimism, the future may seem dark. No matter. Consider this moving incident discovered by Alistair Cooke in the records of the Connecticut House of Representatives:

> The time was the 19th of May, 1780. The place was Hartford, Connecticut. The day has gone down in New England history as a terrible foretaste of Judgment Day. For at noon the skies turned from blue to gray and by mid-afternoon had blackened over so densely that, in that religious age, men fell on their knees and begged a final blessing before the end came. The Connecticut House of Representatives was in session. And as some men fell down and others clamored for an immediate adjournment, the Speaker of the House, one Colonel Davenport, came to his feet. He silenced them and said these words: "The Day of Judgment is either approaching or it is not. If it is not, there is no cause for adjournment. If it is, I choose to be found doing my duty. I wish, therefore, that candles may be brought."[34]

Evangelicals must do their duty. They must take the lead to determine America's future. Over the years, the familiar voice of Billy Graham has forcefully reminded hearers that "This is your hour of decision." By the same token, in this closing decade of the twentieth century, this is America's decade of decision. If God allows, we may have ten more years to make our national choice.

The coming civil war is at hand. The soldiers of decadence and ruin are marching, grimly determined to reshape the nation in their own image. They can be stopped—but not without a fight. Who will respond to God's trumpet blast to battle? This is the evangelical hour. The time to choose has come.

History awaits your decision—or the United States awaits God's judgment.

Notes

1. Alistair Cooke, *America* (New York: Alfred A. Knopf, 1974), 136.

2. Proverbs 14:12.

3. Ann Arbor, Michigan: Servant Publications, 1989, 9-11.

4. Quoted in Steve Halliday and Al Janssen, eds., *Carl Henry at His Best* (Portland: Multnomah Press, 1990), 46.

5. Henry J. Hyde, "The Culture War," *National Review*, 30 April 1990, 25.

6. Sunday, 15 July 1990.

7. Aleksandr Solzhenitsyn in an interview with David Aikman in *Time*, 24 July 1989, 60.

8. *Cultural Conservatism: Toward a New National Agenda* (Washington, D.C.: Free Congress Research and Education Foundation), 4.

9. Eidsmoe, 295.

10. Paul Weyrich, memorandum dated 18 April 1990, Free Congress Foundation.

11. Solzhenitsyn, 60.

12. Bruce L. Shelley, *The Gospel and the American Dream.* (Portland: Multnomah Press, 1989), 109.

13. Josh McDowell, "The Gap Widens," *Eternity*, June 1987, 15.

14. 1 Corinthians 1:20-21; 2:6-8.

15. Ephesians 6:12.

16. Galatians 3:28.

17. Terri Graves Taylor, "Genesis," 9 April 1990, 6f.

18. See Christina Hoff Sommers, "Feminism and the College Curriculum," *Imprimis*, June 1990, 1.

19. *NAE Washington Insight* newsletter, January 1984. *NAE Washington Insight* was born in March, 1979, as an evangelical equivalent of the *Kiplinger Washington Letter* for businessmen. It tries to make clear by disseminating pertinent and accurate information what government is doing (or threatening to do). One small-town pastor said the newsletter was ". . . long overdue. It is like having a hotline to Washington."

20. Speech given by Weigel, President of Washington's Ethics and Public Policy Center, at *NAE Washington Insight* Briefing, 1990.

21. Weyrich, 8.

22. Media bias on the abortion issue was undeniably demonstrated by a 1-4 July 1990 series of articles in the *Los Angeles Times*. We noticed a significant admission along those lines weeks before, when the *Washington Post*'s ombudsman admitted that his paper had not distinguished itself with its biased reporting on pro-life events.

23. Kenneth A. Myers, "Holy Excrement," *Genesis*, 9 April 1990.

24. Reported in the *Washington Post*, 13 October 1987.

25. Rolf Zettersten, "Something Worth Saving Again," *Focus on the Family* magazine, September 1989, 23.

26. Isaiah 5:20, 24.

27. 2 Chronicles 7:14.

28. Halliday and Janssen, 11.

29. Data in this paragraph from *National & International Religion Report*, 30 July 1990, 6.

30. This fact and other data in the immediately following paragraphs are taken from George H. Gallup, Jr., *Religion in America 1990* (Princeton: Princeton Religion Research Center, 1990) and Gallup Poll News Service release dated 27 June 1990.

31. 1 Samuel 17:47.

32. Revelation 3:8.

33. "The Tuned Out Generation," *Time*, 9 July 1990, 64.

34. *Living With Our Differences: Religious Liberty in a Pluralistic Society*, First Liberty Institute (Boston: Learning Connections Publishers, Inc., 1990) upper elementary edition, 183.

Epilogue

Interviewer: Do politicians take evangelicals seriously these days?

Doug Wead: I think they kind of treat the evangelical movement like a seven-foot tall high schooler who can't play basketball. If he ever learns how to play, he's going to be awesome. In the meantime, they'll do everything they can to take advantage of his awkwardness. . . .

Evangelicals can generate more mail, more phone calls, than any other group. We've always known that. Our predecessors told us that. Evangelicals have the numbers. But . . .[1]

In my judgment, Doug Wead was on target with his off-the-cuff but candid response. Who should know better? An evangelical himself, Doug was an advisor to presidential candidate George Bush, a member of his White House transition team, and then for almost two years, special assistant to the president in public liaison.

We must admit that evangelicals have been awkward. The sole political act of literally millions of individual Christians—aside from voting—has been to sign a certain anonymous petition and mail it to the FCC to protest Madalyn Murray O'Hair's efforts "to get all religious broadcasting off the air." Now, there are a few small problems with that petition. First, O'Hair was never involved in it. Second, it was never designed to remove religious broadcasting from the airwaves. Third, the petition was resolved satisfactorily by the FCC in August 1975. That's not a typo—1975 is the correct year.

Those sincere Christians were misinformed. Somebody lied to them. The FCC never has been able to turn off the spigot from which the petitions flowed. The total is climbing beyond 25 million, taxpayers' dollars are being wasted in handling the mail, and the useless petitions are becoming landfill.

On the other hand, evangelicals in the '80s gave promise of becoming awesome. Serious candidates for public office were emerging from prayer meetings rather than smoke-filled rooms. Telephones rang off the hook on Capitol Hill when critical issues were being debated in Congress. Church governmental concerns committees were providing dependable educational materials, so that their people could determine how to vote intelligently. If certain members of Congress voted against funding for religious child care while voting for funding of homoerotic art (as actually happened in the 101st Congress), evangelicals were learning about it before election day, when the information was particularly valuable. In many states and localities, evangelical volunteers flooded the political parties and influenced their policies.

One of these days, that evangelical seven-footer will become coordinated and fulfill his potential. The elections of 1980, 1984, and 1988 felt the impact of an identifiable evangelical vote. No longer could the media treat evangelicals like the Rodney Dangerfield ("I don't get no respect") of American politics.

Suppose knowledgeable evangelicals, given a clear choice in an off-year Senate election, turn out a significantly larger vote than the rest of the population? Assuming Gallup's figure that 33 percent of the people are evangelical, suppose half of evangelicals voted while only 35 percent of non-evangelicals did. Then evangelicals would cast 40 percent of the total votes, rather than their usual 33 percent if all groups voted at the same rate. With such an advantage, "their" challenger could unseat an incumbent and become a United States Senator.

Consider a future presidential election where one candidate genuinely supports culturally conservative values while the other turns his back on evangelical concerns. Let's assume more modest statistics than Gallup's, suggesting that evangelicals represent only 20 percent of the electorate. If 75 percent of evangelicals cast ballots while only half of the non-evangelicals did, evangelicals would control over 27 percent of the total vote, not just their usual 20 percent.

Once more, cutting the margin even more finely, project the impact of a 60 percent evangelical vote against 50 percent for the rest. Then evangelicals would own 23 percent of the total, not just 20 percent. That extra 3 percent may not seem like much, but if most of it were cast for the loser, in 1960, it would have given Richard Nixon the victory over John F. Kennedy; in 1968 it would have pushed Hubert Humphrey past Richard Nixon; and in 1976 it would have returned Gerald Ford to the Oval Office over Jimmy Carter.

There is no doubt that evangelical Christians **can** win the culture war, by the sheer weight of their vote. Whether they **will** win depends upon their spiritual leaders, for "if the trumpet does not sound a clear call, who will get ready for battle?"[2] For those leaders, Carl Henry has the final word:

Can Western civilization escape inner chaos and self-destruction if it faces the future without a significant role for transcendent justice and the revealed will of God? If you think not—as I think not—then your Christian commitment imposes upon you a heavy duty to share in the present effort to preserve the American republic and to warn and instruct all the modern powers that are marching off the map to join once-great nations of antiquity in their oblivion.[3]

Notes

1. Stephen Strang, interview in *Charisma and Christian Life*, July 1990, 80.

2. 1 Corinthians 14:8.

3. Quoted in Steve Halliday and Al Janssen, eds., *Carl Henry at His Best* (Portland: Multnomah Press, 1990), 46.

Appendix I

Political Activity by Clergymen

Alan P. Dye, Esq.
Washington, D.C.

The IRS treatment of legislative and political activities by clergymen and organizations exempt from tax under Section 501(c)(3) of the Internal Revenue Code of 1954 (the Code) is subject to changing IRS interpretations, and it is dangerous to generalize based upon specific cases. Nevertheless, certain general principles may be relied upon with reasonable certainty. These are summarized below, along with the answers to some frequently asked questions.

Law and Regulations

An organization is exempt from tax under Section 501(c)(3) if it is:

". . . a corporation, . . . fund, or foundation, organized and operated exclusively for religious, charitable, scientific, testing for public safety, literary, or educational purposes,

. . . no part of the net earnings of which inures to the benefit of any private shareholder or individual, no substantial part of the activities of which is carrying on propaganda, or otherwise attempting to influence legislation (except as provided in subsection [h]), and which does not participate in, or intervene in (including the publishing and distributing of statements), any political campaign on behalf of any candidate for public office."

It is apparent from the language of the statute that an *organization* exempt from tax under Section 501(c)(3) may undertake *no activity whatever* on behalf of or in opposition to any candidate for public office—federal, state, or local. This is an absolute prohibition.

Legislative activities, as contrasted to political activities, are permissible for such an organization. However, the statute specifically prescribes that no *substantial* part of the activities of such an organization may be devoted to activities intended to influence legislation.

The IRS regulations under Section 501(c)(3) elaborate on the general statutory requirements as follows:

(3) *Authorization of legislative or political activities.* An organization is not organized exclusively for one or more exempt purposes if its articles expressly empower it:

(i) To devote more than an insubstantial part of its activities to attempting to influence legislation by propaganda or otherwise; or

(ii) Directly or indirectly to participate in, or intervene in (including the publishing or distributing of statements), any political campaign on behalf of or in opposition to any candidate for public office; or

(iii) To have objectives and to engage in activities which characterize it as an "action" organization as defined in paragraph (c)(3) of this section.

Sections 1.501(c)(3)-1(b)(3)(i) and (ii) of the above regulation merely restate Section 501(c)(3) and its prohibition of political activity and limitations on legislative activity, but subsection (iii) expands the limitations placed upon charitable or educational organizations to preclude Section 501(c)(3) status for so-called "action" organizations, which are defined to include any organization which contacts or urges the public to contact legislators regarding legislation or which itself advocates the adoption or rejection of legislation.

The statute does not define the term "substantial" for purposes of determining whether an organization qualifies under Section 501(c)(3). Court cases have held that an organization may devote at least 5 percent of its activities to lobbying without losing its tax-favored status, and that an organization devoting more than 20 percent of its activities to lobbying does not qualify. Organizations devoting between 5 and 20 percent of their activities to such pursuits are in an area of uncertainty. The IRS has never accepted the applicability of any specific percentage to determine the substantiality of any organization's legislative activity.

In 1976, Code Section 501(h) was enacted to relieve some of this uncertainty. That section sets forth a procedure whereby an organization may elect to expend a specified portion of its budget for legislative activities without any adverse effect upon its tax-exempt status. The amount of such activity is computed on a statutorily prescribed sliding scale. As an example, an organization whose total expenditures on all exempt purposes are less than $500,000 per year may devote up to 20 percent of such expenditures to lobbying without paying any tax, and up to 30 percent without losing its tax-exempt status. Expenditures exceeding 20 percent, but less than 30 percent, are subject to a special tax, but will not adversely affect tax-exempt status.

Under Section 501(h), one-quarter of the allowable expenditure amount may be devoted to so-called "grass-roots lobbying," defined as attempts to influence the general public regarding legislation. Organizations not electing under Section 501(h) are subject to the old rules. In either case, permissible lobbying must be in the public interest.

Section 501(h) may be elected by most organizations qualifying for tax exemption under Section 501(c)(3) of the Internal Revenue Code. However, while the bill was being considered by Congress, there were those in the church community who believed that churches are not subject to the prohibitions against lobbying in any respect. These organizations believed that to include churches and integrated auxiliaries of churches in the relief legislation would imply that the government had the right to revoke their tax exemptions if they engaged in legislative activity. Since they do not believe that this is true, the organizations lobbied for a provision excluding them from the benefits of 501(h). The result is that churches, integrated auxiliaries of churches, and members of affiliated groups in which one or more members are churches or integrated auxiliaries of churches are not eligible to elect the provision of Section 501(h). Religious institutions which are not churches or integrated auxiliaries can make this election.

The requirements of the statute may thus be summarized as follows: An organization carrying on public affairs activities may qualify for exemption from tax under Section 501(c)(3) and receive charitable contributions under Section 170(a) if its activities are educational, charitable or religious; if it does not exceed the limitations imposed on lobbying and propaganda expenditures imposed by Section 501(c)(3) and/or Section 501(h); and if it engages in no activity intended to influence the election or defeat of any political candidate.

Federal elections are governed by Title 2 of the U.S. Code Section 431, *et seq.*, comprising the Federal Election Campaign Act of 1971, as amended. The election laws prohibit contributions or expenditures in connection with any federal campaign by any corporation. Since many churches and charities are incorporated, the prohibition extends to many such organizations. It should be noted that this prohibition extends only to "contributions" and "expenditures." Thus, directly or indirectly, a corporation must *spend money* in support of or opposition to a candidate before a violation can be found. Activity by a minister outside working hours would not constitute a contribution by his church, though political advocacy on church time might. Use of church facilities for a political purpose by a candidate or committee may be the equivalent of a contribution, but merely allowing a visiting politician to deliver a sermon or read Scripture would not.

Discussion

1. Endorsements

   a. *Can a clergyman or office of a nonprofit tax-exempt organization publicly endorse a candidate for public office?*

   Neither the federal tax statutes nor the federal election law place impediments upon individuals expressing their election choices. The fact that a clergyman is employed by a tax-exempt organization does not destroy his personal constitutional right to political expression, and such an individual may personally endorse or oppose candidates for office without endangering the tax-exempt status of the organization by which he is employed.

   b. *Can it be done from the premises or pulpit of the tax-exempt organization?*

   Yes. There is no instance of which we are aware in which the Internal Revenue Service or the Federal Election Commission has sought to take adverse action against a church solely because its minister endorsed a candidate from the pulpit. However, a clergyman should not make a regular practice of endorsing candidates from the pulpit, lest his personal position be attributed to his church, and on those occasions when he does do so, he should make it clear to his congregation that the endorsement is a personal one and not that of the institution.

   c. *Can the church or "organization" endorse a candidate?*

   The federal election law prohibits the expenditure of corporate funds in an attempt to influence an election. If the endorsement does not involve such a corporate expenditure, it would be permissible under the election law.

However, Section 501(c)(3) of the Internal Revenue Code prohibits any direct or indirect participation in political campaigns by a charitable or religious organization. This prohibition is broader than that of the election law, and extends to more than the mere expenditure of funds. Therefore, a charitable *organization* (including a church) which endorses a candidate for public office would be participating in a political campaign and would endanger its tax-exempt status.

We are aware of no instances in which the Internal Revenue Service has sought to revoke the tax-exempt status of a church merely because the church has endorsed a political candidate. However, this is probably due to the traditional timidity of the IRS in the face of organized religion, and such a policy could be changed at any time.

d. *Can the clergyman or nonprofit organization leader/officer lend his name to political advertisements and have his title listed under his name for identification purposes?*

Just as there is no prohibition against an individual employed by a tax-exempt organization engaging in political activity, there is no prohibition against the candidate using the individual's identification with such an organization if it is helpful in his candidacy. Clergymen who work on their own time in political campaigns may be identified by their organizational titles.

2. Voter Registration and Education

a. *Can a Section 501(c)(3) organization encourage or conduct voter registration or voter education activities among church members or on the nonprofit premises?*

Yes. The IRS has ruled that even private foundations may support voter education drives. T.D. Release K-87, May 11, 1969. In this respect, IRS Revenue Ruling 78-248, states as follows:

"Certain 'voter education' activities conducted in the nonpartisan manner may not constitute prohibited political activity under section 501(c)(3) of the Code. Other so-called 'voter education' activities, however may be proscribed by the statute."

This revenue ruling contains a number of examples of situations illustrative of the rules as applied by the IRS.

In one example, an organization compiled and made generally available to the public voting records of all members of Congress. The publication contained no editorial opinion, and its contents did not imply approval or disapproval of the members' voting records. The IRS held that such activity is not prohibited to a Section 501(c)(3) organization.

In another situation an organization was found to qualify as a Section 501(c)(3) organization even though it published a "voter's guide" containing the opinions of various candidates for political office on a wide variety of issues. It is important to note that the issues were selected solely on the basis of their importance and interest to the electorate as a whole. Candidates' positions were ascertained through answers to a questionnaire sent to all candidates.

Important distinctions may be drawn from a third example in which the same sort of questionnaire was sent to candidates in order to prepare a voters' guide, but the questionnaire was structured in such a way that it evidenced bias on certain issues. The organization was held not to qualify for tax-exempt status.

b. *Must voter registration activities be nonpartisan?*

Yes.

c. *Can the organization spend money for paying registration organizers, or for mailing out registration forms?*

Yes, if the registration is nonpartisan.

3. Candidate Appearances

a. *Can candidates speak on the premises of a Section 501(c)(3) organization?*

The Internal Revenue Service has never to our knowledge attempted to revoke the tax-exempt status of an organization which has allowed political candidates to speak on the premises. It is fairly clear that there is no problem with such practice if all candidates are allowed to speak, rather than merely those endorsed by the leaders of the institution. This is consistent with revenue rulings dealing with broadcasting stations, in which it has been held that providing reasonable air time to all legally qualified candidates for election to public office does not constitute participation in a political campaign. See Rev. Rel. 74-574, 1974-2 C.B. 160.

The question is a closer one if only certain candidates are allowed to address the group with political speeches. It could, of course, be argued that allowing a candidate to speak involves no expenditure or endorsement by the organization or that purely internal communications do not constitute intervention in a political campaign. Further, as we have noted, we know of no instance in which an organization has lost its tax-exempt status for such activities. Nevertheless, more care and consideration should be given to such an activity than to an activity where all candidates are provided with the opportunity to speak.

Of course, candidates and public officials retain their rights to religious expression. Ministers should be safe in introducing a candidate present in the congregation at a service, and candidates may be allowed to deliver sermons and read Scripture.

b. *Can a public incumbent office holder speak on the premises or from the pulpit?*

Yes, though if such office holders are candidates, the same considerations apply as are discussed above.

c. *Can an organization exempt from tax under Section 501(c)(3) operate forums where all candidates for a particular office come and speak?*

Though the Internal Revenue Service has apparently never ruled on this exact question, such an activity is consistent with other IRS rulings. See, for instance, Revenue Ruling 74-574, *supra*, involving appearances by candidates on television stations operated by religious and educational groups. See, also, Revenue Ruling 66-256, 1966-2 C.B. 210, in which an organization was held to qualify for Section 501(c)(3) status where it conducted public forums at which elections and debates on social, political, and international matters are presented.

4. Fund Raising

Can funds be raised at religious services for campaign contributions to candidates, contributions to political parties, or contributions for a legislative battle or moral or educational issue campaign?

An organization may qualify for Section 501(c)(3) status so long as it does not devote a *substantial* portion of its activities to propaganda or legislative activities. Collecting money at a church service does not involve an expenditure of funds which could under any circumstances amount to a substantial expenditure. Therefore, allowing fundraising for lobbying campaigns at church services incurs no significant expense.

In contrast, raising money for a candidate or political party would constitute indirect participation in a political campaign. Since the prohibition on such activities is absolute, such an activity could result in the loss of tax-exempt status.

5. Mailing Lists

Can an organization exempt from tax under Section 501(c)(3) loan or rent its mailing list to an organization carrying on legislative activities or to a candidate or political committee for campaign fund raising?

Both the Federal Election Commission and the Internal Revenue Service would react adversely to a loan of an organization's mailing list for use in a political campaign. Such an activity would constitute a corporate political expenditure to the extent that corporate funds had been used to develop the membership list. It would also constitute participation in a political campaign for purposes of Section 501(c)(3).

The loan of a mailing list to a "legislative" organization must be analyzed using different principles. The election law would not apply since that statute applies only to political activities rather than legislative ones. The loan could be considered a legislative expenditure to the extent of the cost of providing it, but in any event would be considered such an expenditure only to the extent of any additional cost incurred by the corporation. Presumably, such additional costs would be very slight and would only in a very unusual circumstance result in substantial expenditure.

It is clear that both political candidates and parties and legislative organizations can *buy* mailing lists from charitable organizations. No problem would exist in any of the above cases if the list were rented at its fair market value (the value at which it is rented to other organizations, if at all) to either a political organization or a legislative organization.

We have attempted to deal in general summary form with problems which commonly arise. The reader should recognize, however, that the tax effect of political or legislative activity on a church or charity depends on the precise facts of the particular case. Each church should consult its own counsel with respect to its specific activities.

Revised April 1990

Appendix II

Resources to Get You Started

The easiest way to get in touch with the party of your choice is through its office in your county. Look for the Democratic Party of _____ County or Republican Party of _____ County in the white pages of your telephone book. A phone call is always in order, but tens of thousands of volunteers have simply walked into their party's headquarters and engaged in a friendly conversation—in most cases with another volunteer. Paid staff at the county level, where it exists, is likely to be very small or perhaps only part-time.

On the following pages are listed the addresses (as of press time) for the national and all state Democratic and Republican parties in the nation.

Democratic Party National Committees

Democratic National Committee
430 South Capitol Street SE
Washington, DC 20003
(202) 863-8000

Democratic Congressional Campaign Committee
430 South Capitol Street SE
Washington, DC 20003
(202) 863-1500

Democratic Senatorial Campaign Committee
430 South Capitol Street SE
Washington, DC 20003
(202) 224-2447

Democratic State Parties

Alabama Democratic Party
4120 Third Avenue South
Birmingham, AL 35222

Alaska Democratic Party
P.O. Box 10-4199
Anchorage, AK 99510

Arizona Democratic Party
1509 N. Central
Suite 100
Phoenix, AZ 85004

Arkansas Democratic Party
1300 West Capitol
Little Rock, AR 72201

California Democratic Party
329 Bryant Street
Suite 3C
San Francisco, CA 94107

Colorado Democratic Party
1600 Downing Street
Sixth Floor
Denver, CO 80207

Connecticut Democratic Party
634 Asylum Avenue
Hartford, CT 06105

Delaware Democratic Party
609 West Newport Pike
Wilmington, DE 19804

D.C. Democratic Party
1012 14th Street NW
Suite 806
Washington, DC 20005

Florida Democratic Party·
P.O. Box 1758
Tallahassee, FL 32302

Georgia Democratic Party
1100 Spring Street
Suite 350
Atlanta, GA 30367

Hawaii Democratic Party
50 South Beretania St.
Suite C-101B
Honolulu, HI 96813

Idaho Democratic Party
Box 445
Boise, ID 83701

Democratic Party of Illinois
1007 North 7th Street
Springfield, IL 62706

Indiana Democratic Party
1 North Capitol
Indianapolis, IN 46204

Iowa Democratic Party
2116 Grand Avenue
Des Moines, IA 50312

Kansas Democratic Party
P.O. Box 1914
Topeka, KS 66601

Kentucky Democratic Party
P.O. Box 694
Frankfort, KY 40602

Louisiana Democratic Party
3114 College Drive
Suite J
Baton Rouge, LA 70821

Maine Democratic Party
P.O. Box 5258
Augusta, ME 04332-5258

Maryland Democratic Party
224 Main Street
Annapolis, MD 21401

Massachusetts Democratic Party
45 Bromfield Street
7th Floor
Boston, MA 02108

Michigan Democratic Party
606 Townsend
Lansing, MI 48933

Minnesota Democratic Farmer Labor Party
525 Park Street
Suite 100
St. Paul, MN 55103

Mississippi Democratic Party
P.O. Box 1583
Jackson, MS 39205

Missouri Democratic Party
P.O. Box 719
Jefferson City, MO 65102

Montana Democratic Party
P.O. Box 802
Helena, MT 59624

Nebraska Democratic Party
715 South 14th Street
Lincoln, NE 68508

Nevada Democratic Party
953 East Sahara
Süite 236
Las Vegas, NV 89104

New Hampshire Democratic Party
922 Elm Street
Suite 210
Manchester, NH 03101

New Jersey Democratic Party
150 West State Street
Trenton, NJ 08608

New Mexico Democratic Party
315 8th Street, SW
Albuquerque, NM 87102

New York Democratic Party
60 E. 42nd Street
Suite 1801
New York, NY 10165

North Carolina Democratic Party
P.O. Box 12196
Raleigh, NC 27605

North Dakota Democratic Party
1902 East Divide Avenue
Bismarck, ND 58501

Ohio Democratic Party
88 East Broad Street
Suite 1920
Columbus, OH 43215

Oklahoma Democratic Party
116 E. Sheridan Street
Suite G 100
Oklahoma City, OK 73104

Oregon Democratic Party
P.O. Box 15057
Salem, OR 97756

Pennsylvania Democratic Party
510 North Third Street
Harrisburg, PA 17101

Rhode Island Democratic Party
1991 Smith Street
North Providence, RI 02911

South Carolina Democratic Party
P.O. Box 5965
Columbia, SC 29250

South Dakota Democratic Party
P.O. Box 737
Sioux Falls, SD 57101

Tennessee Democratic Party
431 11th Avenue North
Nashville, TN 37203

Texas Democratic Party
815 Brazos Street
Suite 200
Austin, TX 78701

Utah Democratic Party
472 Bearcat Drive
Salt Lake City, UT 84115

Vermont Democratic Party
P.O. Box 336
Montpelier, VT 05602

Virginia Democratic Party
1001 East Broad Street
Suite LL25
Richmond, VA 23219

Washington Democratic Party
P.O. Box 4027
Seattle, WA 98104

West Virginia Democratic Party
405 Capitol Street
Suite 501
Charleston, WV 25301

Wisconsin Democratic Party
126 South Franklin Street
Madison, WI 53703-3494

Wyoming Democratic Party
P.O. Box 2036
Cheyenne, WY 82003

Republican Party National Committees

Republican National Committee
310 First Street, SE
Washington, DC 20003
(202) 863-8500

National Republican Senatorial Committee
440 First Street, NW
Washington, DC 20002
(202) 675-6000

National Republican Congressional Committee
320 First Street, SE
Washington, DC 20003
(202) 479-7000

Republican State Parties

Alabama Republican Executive Committee
P.O. Box 320800
Birmingham, AL 35232-0800

Republican Party of Alaska
750 East Fireweed Lane
Suite 102
Anchorage, AK 99503

Arizona Republican State Committee
3501 North 24th Street
Phoenix, AZ 85016-6607

Republican Party of Arkansas
One Riverfront Place
Suite 550
North Little Rock, AR 72114

California Republican Party
1903 West Magnolia
Burbank, CA 91506

Republican State Central Committee of Colorado
1275 Tremont Place
Denver, CO 80204

Connecticut Republican State Central Committee
78 Oak Street
Hartford, CT 06106

Delaware Republican State Committee
2 Mill Road
Suite 108
Wilmington, DE 19806

District of Columbia Republican Committee
440 First St., N.W.
4th Floor
Washington, DC 20001

Republican State Executive Committee of Florida
P.O. Box 311
Tallahassee, FL 32302

Georgia Republican Party
3091 Maple Drive, NE
Suite 315
Atlanta, GA 30305

Republican Party of Hawaii
100 N. Beretania St.
Suite 203
Honolulu, HI 96817

Idaho Republican State Central Committee
P.O. Box 2267
Boise, ID 83701

Illinois Republican State Central Committee
223 South Third Street
Springfield, IL 62701

Indiana Republican State Central Committee
200 South Meridian
Suite 400
Indianapolis, IN 46225

Republican State Central Committee of Iowa
521 East Locust Street
Des Moines, IA 50309

Kansas Republican State Committee
214 West 6th Street
Topeka, KS 66603

Republican Party of Kentucky
P.O. Box 1068
Frankfort, KY 40602

The Republican Party of Louisiana
650 North 6th Street
Baton Rouge, LA 70802

Maine Republican Party
24 Stone Street
Augusta, ME 04330

Republican State Central Committee of Maryland
1623 Forest Drive
Suite 400
Annapolis, MD 21403

Massachusetts Republican State Committee
#9 Galen Street
Suite 320
Watertown, MA 02172

Michigan Republican State Committee
2121 E. Grand River
Lansing, MI 48912

Independent Republicans of Minnesota
8030 Cedar Avenue
Suite 220
Bloomington, MN 55425

Mississippi Republican Party
P.O. Box 60
Jackson, MS 39205

Missouri Republican State Committee
P.O. Box 73
Jefferson City, MO 65102

Montana Republican State Central Committee
1425 Helena Avenue
Helena, MT 59601

Nebraska Republican State Central Committee
421 South 9th Street
Suite 233
Lincoln, NE 68508

Republican State Central Committee of Nevada
6114 West Charleston
Las Vegas, NV 89102

New Hampshire Republican State Committee
134 North Main Street
Concord, NH 03301

New Jersey Republican State Committee
310 West State Street
Trenton, NJ 08618

Republican Party of New Mexico
P.O. Box 36900
Albuquerque, NM 87176

New York Republican State Committee
315 State Street
Albany, NY 12210

North Carolina Republican Executive Committee
1410 Hillsborough St.
P.O. Box 12905
Raleigh, NC 27605

North Dakota Republican State Committee
P.O. Box 1917
Bismarck, ND 58502

Republican State Central And Executive Committee of Ohio
172 East State Street
Fourth Floor
Columbus, OH 43215

Republican State Committee of Oklahoma
4031 N. Lincoln Blvd.
Oklahoma City, OK 73105

Oregon Republican Party
9900 S.W. Greenburg Road
Suite 150
Portland, OR 97223

Republican State Committee of Pennsylvania
P.O. Box 1624
Harrisburg, PA 17101

Rhode Island Republican State Central Committee
400 Smith Street
Providence, RI 02908

The South Carolina Republican Party
P.O. Box 21765
Columbia, SC 29221

South Dakota Republican State Central Committee
P.O. Box 1099
Pierre, SD 57501

Tennessee Republican State Executive Committee
2817 West End Avenue
Nashville, TN 37203

Republican Party of Texas
211 East 7th Street
Suite 620
Austin, TX 78701

Utah Republican State Central Committee
637 East 400 South
Salt Lake City, UT 84102

Vermont Republican State Committee
P.O. Box 70
Montpelier, VT 05602

Republican Party of Virginia
115 East Grace Street
Richmond, VA 23219

Republican State Committee of Washington
Nine Lake Bellevue Drive
Suite 203
Bellevue, WA 98005

Republican State Executive Committee of West Virginia
101 Dee Drive
Charleston, WV 25311

Republican Party of Wisconsin
P.O. Box 31
Madison, WI 53701

Wyoming Republican State Committee
P.O. Box 241
Casper, WY 82602

Appendix III

Ronald Reagan's "Evil Empire" Speech

Citrus Crown Ballroom
Sheraton Twin Towers Hotel
Orlando, Florida
March 8, 1983

Those of you in the National Association of Evangelicals are known for your spiritual and humanitarian work. And I would be especially remiss if I didn't discharge right now one personal debt of gratitude. Thank you for your prayers. Nancy and I have felt their presence many times in many ways. And believe me, for us they've made all the difference. The other day in the East Room of the White House at a meeting there, someone asked me whether I was aware of all the people out there who were praying for the president and I had to say, "Yes, I am. I've felt it. I believe in intercessory prayer." But I couldn't help but say to that questioner after he'd asked the question that—or at least say to them that if sometimes when he was praying he got a busy signal it was just me in there ahead of him.

I think I understand how Abraham Lincoln felt when he said, "I have been driven many times to my knees by the overwhelming conviction that I had nowhere else to go."

From the joy and the good feeling of this conference, I go to a political reception. Now, I don't know why, but that bit of scheduling reminds me of a story which I'll share with you. An evangelical minister and a politician arrived at heaven's gate one day together. And St. Peter, after doing all the necessary formalities, took them in hand to show them where their quarters would be. And he took them to a small single room with a bed, a chair, and a table and said this was for the clergyman. And the politician was a little worried about what might be in store for him. And he couldn't believe it then when St. Peter stopped in front of a beautiful mansion with lovely grounds, many servants and told him that these would be his quarters. And he couldn't help but ask, "But wait, how—there's something wrong—how do I get this mansion while that good and holy man gets a single room?"

And St. Peter said, "You have to understand how things are up here. We've got thousands and thousands of clergy. You're the first politician who ever made it."

But I don't want to contribute to the stereotype. So I tell you there are a great many God-fearing, dedicated, noble men and women in public life, present company included. And yes, we need your help to keep us ever mindful of the ideas and the principles that brought us into the public arena in the first place. The basis of those ideas and principles is a commitment to freedom and personal liberty that, itself, is grounded in the much deeper realization that freedom prospers only where the blessings of God are avidly sought and humbly accepted.

The American experiment in democracy rests on this insight. Its discovery was the great triumph of our founding fathers, voiced by William Penn when he said, "If we will not be governed by God, we must be governed by tyrants." Explaining the inalienable rights of men, Jefferson said, "The God who gave us life, gave us liberty at the same time." And it was George Washington who said that "of all the dispositions and habits which lead to political prosperity, religion and morality are indispensable supports."

And finally, that shrewdest of all observers of American democracy, Alexis de Tocqueville, put it eloquently after he had gone on a search for the secret of America's greatness and genius—and he said:

> "Not until I went into the Churches of America and heard her pulpits aflame with righteousness did I understand the greatness and the genius of America. America is good. And if America ever ceases to be good, America will cease to be great."

Well, I am pleased to be here today with you who are keeping America great by keeping her good. Only through your work and prayers and those of millions of others can we hope to survive this perilous century and keep alive this experiment in liberty, this last, best hope of man.

I want you to know that this administration is motivated by a political philosophy that sees the greatness of America in you, her people, and in your families, churches, neighborhoods, communities—the institutions that foster and nourish values like concern for others and respect for the rule of law under God.

Now, I don't have to tell you that this puts us in opposition to, or at least out of step with, a prevailing attitude of many who have turned to a modern-day secularism, discarding the tried and time-tested values upon which our civilization is based. No matter how well intentioned, their value system is radically different from that of most Americans. And while they proclaim that they are freeing us from superstitions of the past, they have taken upon themselves the job of superintending us by government rule and regulation. Sometimes their voices are louder than ours, but they are not yet a majority.

An example of that vocal superiority is evident in a controversy now going on in Washington. And since I'm involved, I've been waiting to hear from the parents of young America. How far are they willing to go in giving to government their prerogatives as parents?

Let me state the case as briefly and simply as I can. An organization of citizens sincerely motivated and deeply concerned about the increase in illegitimate births and abortions involving girls well below the age of consent sometime ago established a nationwide network of clinics to offer help to these girls and hopefully alleviate this situation.

Now, again, let me say, I do not fault their intent. However, in their well-intentioned effort, these clinics have decided to provide advice and birth control drugs and devices to underage girls without the knowledge of their parents.

For some years now, the federal government has helped with funds to subsidize these clinics. In providing for this, the Congress decreed that every effort would be made to maximize parental participation. Nevertheless, the drugs and devices are prescribed without getting parental consent or giving notification after they've done so. Girls termed "sexually active"—and that has replaced the word "promiscuous"—are given this help in order to prevent illegitimate birth or abortion.

We have ordered clinics receiving federal funds to notify the parents such help has been given. One of the nation's leading newspapers created the term "squeal rule" in editorializing against us for doing this and we're being criticized for violating the privacy of young people. A judge has recently granted an injunction against an enforcement of our rule.

I've watched TV panel shows discuss this issue, seen columnists pontificating on our error, but no one seems to mention morality as playing a part in the subject of sex.

Is all of Judeo-Christian tradition wrong? Are we to believe that something so sacred can be looked upon as a purely physical thing with no potential for emotional and psychological harm? And isn't it the parents' right to give counsel and advice to keep their children from making mistakes that may affect their entire lives?

Many of us in government would like to know what parents think about this intrusion in their family by government. We're going to fight in the courts. The right of parents and the rights of family take precedence over those of Washington-based bureaucrats and social engineers.

But the fight against parental notification is really only one example of many attempts to water down traditional values and even abrogate the original terms of American democracy. Freedom prospers when religion is vibrant and the rule of law under God is acknowledged. When our founding fathers passed the First Amendment they sought to protect churches from government interference. They never intended to construct a wall of hostility between government and the concept of religious belief itself.

The evidence of this permeates our history and our government. The Declaration of Independence mentions the Supreme Being no less than four times. "In God We Trust" is engraved on our coinage. The Supreme Court opens its proceedings with a religious invocation. And the members of Congress open their sessions with a prayer. I just happen to believe the schoolchildren of the United States are entitled to the same privileges as Supreme Court judges and congressmen. Last year, I sent the Congress a constitutional amendment to restore prayer to public schools. Already this session, there's growing bipartisan support for the amendment and I am calling on the Congress to act speedily to pass it and to let our children pray.

Perhaps some of you read recently about the Lubbock school case where a judge actually ruled that it was unconstitutional for a school district to give equal treatment to religious and nonreligious student groups, even when the group meetings were being held during the students' own time. The First Amendment never intended to require government to discriminate against religious speech.

Senators Denton and Hatfield have proposed legislation in the Congress on the whole question of prohibiting discrimination against religious forms of student speech. Such legislation could go far to restore freedom of religious speech for public school students. And I hope the

Congress considers these bills quickly. And with your help, I think it's possible we could also get the constitutional amendment through the Congress this year.

More than a decade ago, a Supreme Court decision literally wiped off the books of fifty states statutes protecting the rights of unborn children. Abortion on demand now takes the lives of up to 1.5 million unborn children a year. Human life legislation ending this tragedy will some day pass the Congress and you and I must never rest until it does. Unless and until it can be proven that the unborn child is not a living entity, its right to life, liberty, and the pursuit of happiness must be protected.

You may remember that when abortion on demand began many of you warned that the practice would lead to a decline in respect for human life, that the philosophical premises used to justify abortion on demand would ultimately be used to justify other attacks on the sacredness of human life, infanticide, or mercy killing. Tragically enough, those warnings proved all too true: only last year a court permitted the death sentence by starvation of a handicapped infant.

I have directed the Health and Human Services Department to make clear to every health care facility in the United States that the Rehabilitation Act of 1973 protects all handicapped persons against discrimination based on handicaps, including infants. And we have taken the further step of requiring that each and every recipient of federal funds who provides health care services to infants must post and keep posted in a conspicuous place a notice stating that "discriminatory failure to feed and care for handicapped infants in this facility is prohibited by federal law." It also lists a 24-hour, toll-free number so that nurses and others may report violations in time to save the infant's life.

In addition, recent legislation introduced in the Congress by Representative Henry Hyde of Illinois not only increases restrictions on publicly financed abortions, it also addresses this whole problem of infanticide. I urge the Congress to begin hearings and to adopt legislation that will protect the right of life to all children, including the disabled or handicapped.

Now, I'm sure that you must get discouraged at times, but you've done better than you know, perhaps. There is a great spiritual awakening in America, a renewal of the traditional values that have been the bedrock of America's goodness and greatness. One recent survey by a Washington-based research council concluded that Americans were far more religious than the people of other nations; 95 percent of those surveyed expressed a belief in God and a huge majority believed the Ten Commandments had real meaning in their lives.

And another study has found that an overwhelming majority of Americans disapprove of adultery, teenage sex, pornography, abortion, and hard drugs. And this same study showed a deep reverence for the importance of family ties and religious belief.

I think the items that we've discussed here today must be a key part of the nation's political agenda. For the first time the Congress is openly and seriously debating and dealing with the prayer and abortion issues—and that's enormous progress right there. I repeat: America is in the midst of a spiritual awakening and a moral renewal. And with your biblical keynote, I say today, "Yes, let justice roll on like a river, righteousness like a never failing stream."

Now, obviously, much of this new political and social consensus that I have talked about is based on a positive view of American history, one that takes pride in our country's accomplishments and record. But we must never forget that no government schemes are going to perfect man. We know that living in this world means dealing with what philosophers would call the phenomenology of evil or, as theologians would put it, the doctrine of sin.

There is sin and evil in the world. And we are enjoined by Scripture and the Lord Jesus to oppose it with all our might. Our nation, too, has a legacy of evil with which it must deal. The glory of this land has been its capacity for transcending the moral evils of our past. For example, the long struggle of minority citizens for equal rights, once a source of disunity and civil war, is now a point of pride for all Americans. We must never go back. There is no room for racism, anti-semitism, or other forms of ethnic and racial hatred in this country. I know that you have been horrified, as have I, by the resurgence of some hate groups preaching bigotry and prejudice. Use the mighty voice of your pulpits and the powerful standing of your churches to denounce and isolate these hate groups in our midst. The commandment given us is clear and simple: "Thou shalt love thy neighbor as thyself."

But whatever sad episodes exist in our past, any objective observer must hold a positive view of American history, a history that has been the story of hopes fulfilled and dreams made into reality. Especially in this century, America has kept alight the torch of freedom, not just for ourselves, but for millions of others around the world.

And this brings me to my final point today. During my first press conference as president, in answer to a direct question, I pointed out that, as good Marxists-Leninists, the Soviet leaders have openly and publicly declared that the *only morality they recognize* is that which will further their cause, which is world revolution. I think I should point out, I was only quoting Lenin, their guiding spirit, who said in 1920 that they repudiate all morality that proceeds from supernatural ideas—that is their name for religion—or ideas that are outside class conceptions. Morality is entirely subordinate to the interests of class war. And everything is moral that is necessary for the annihilation of the old, exploiting social order and for uniting the proletariat.

Well, I think the refusal of many influential people to accept this elementary fact of Soviet doctrine illustrates a historical reluctance to see totalitarian powers for what they are. We saw this phenomenon in the 1930s. We see it too often today. This does not mean we should isolate ourselves and refuse to seek an understanding with them. I intend to do everything I can to persuade them of our peaceful intent, to remind them that it was the West that refused to use its nuclear monopoly in the '40s and '50s for territorial gain and which now proposes 50 percent cuts in strategic ballistic missiles and the elimination of an entire class of land-based intermediate range nuclear missiles.

At the same time, however, they must be made to understand we will never compromise our principles and standards. We will never give away our freedom. We will never abandon our belief in God. And we will never stop searching for a genuine peace, but we can assure none of these things America stands for through the so-called nuclear freeze solutions proposed by some.

The truth is that a freeze now would be a very dangerous fraud, for that is merely the illusion of peace. The reality is that we must find peace through strength.

I would agree to a freeze only if we could freeze the Soviets' global desires. A freeze at current levels of weapons would remove any incentive for the Soviets to negotiate seriously in Geneva, and virtually end our chances to achieve the major arms reductions which we have proposed. Instead, they would achieve their objectives through the freeze. A freeze would reward the Soviet Union for its enormous and unparalleled military buildup. It would prevent the essential and long overdue modernization of United States and allied defenses and would leave our aging forces increasingly vulnerable. And an honest freeze would require extensive prior negotiations on the systems and numbers to be limited and on the measures to ensure effective verification and compliance. And the kind of freeze that has been suggested would be virtually impossible to verify. Such a major effort would divert us completely from our current negotiations on achieving substantial reductions.

A number of years ago, I heard a young father, a very prominent young man in the entertainment world, addressing a tremendous gathering in California. It was during the time of the cold war, and communism and our own way of life were very much on people's minds. And he was speaking to that subject. And suddenly, though, I heard him saying, "I love my little girls more than anything—" And I said to myself, "Oh, no, don't. You can't—don't say that." But I had underestimated him. He went on: "I would rather see my little girls die now, still believing in God, than have them grow up under communism and one day die no longer believing in God."

There were thousands of young people in that audience. They came to their feet with shouts of joy. They had instantly recognized the profound truth in what he had said, with regard to the physical and the soul and what was truly important.

Yes, let us pray for the salvation of all of those who live in that totalitarian darkness—pray they will discover the joy of knowing God. But until they do, let us be aware that while they preach the supremacy of the state, declare its omnipotence over individual man, and predict its eventual domination of all peoples on the earth—they are the focus of evil in the modern world. It was C.S. Lewis who, in his unforgettable *Screwtape Letters*, wrote: "The greatest evil is not done now in those sordid 'dens of crime' that Dickens loved to paint. It is not even done in concentration camps and labor camps. In those we see its final result. But it is conceived and ordered (moved, seconded, carried, and minuted) in clear, carpeted, warmed, and well-lighted offices, by quiet men with white collars and cut fingernails and smooth-shaven cheeks who do not need to raise their voice."

Because these "quiet men" do not "raise their voices," because they sometimes speak in soothing tones of brotherhood and peace, because, like other dictators before them, they're always making "their final territorial demand," some would have us accept them at their word and accommodate ourselves to their aggressive impulses. But, if history teaches anything, it teaches that simple-minded appeasement or wishful thinking about our adversaries is folly. It means the betrayal of our past, the squandering of our freedom.

So, I urge you to speak out against those who would place the United States in a position of military and moral inferiority. You know, I've always believed that old Screwtape reserved his best efforts for those of you in the church. So, in your discussions of the nuclear freeze proposals, I urge you to beware the temptation of pride— the temptation of blithely declaring yourselves above it all and label both sides equally at fault, to ignore the facts of history and the aggressive impulses of an evil empire, to simply call the arms race a giant misunderstanding and thereby remove yourself from the struggle between right and wrong and good and evil.

I ask you to resist the attempts of those who would have you withhold your support for our efforts, this administration's efforts, to keep America strong and free, while we negotiate real and verifiable reductions in the world's nuclear arsenals and one day, with God's help, their total elimination.

While America's military strength is important, let me add here that I have always maintained that the struggle now going on for the world will never be decided by bombs or rockets, by armies or military might. The real crisis we face today is a spiritual one; at root, it is a test of moral will and faith.

Whittaker Chambers, the man whose own religious conversion made him a witness to one of the terrible traumas of our time, the Hiss-Chambers case, wrote that the crisis of the Western World exists to the degree in which the West is indifferent to God, the degree to which it collaborates in communism's attempt to make man stand alone without God. And then he said, "For Marxism-Leninism is actually the second oldest faith first proclaimed in the Garden of Eden with the words of temptation, 'Ye shall be as gods.'"

"The Western world can answer this challenge," he wrote, "but only provided that its faith in God and the freedom he enjoins is as great as communism's faith in man."

I believe we shall rise to the challenge. I believe that communism is another sad, bizarre chapter in human history whose last pages even now are being written. I believe this because the source of our strength in the quest for human freedom is not material but spiritual. And because it knows no limitation, it must terrify and ultimately triumph over those who would enslave their fellow man. For in the words of Isaiah: "He giveth power to the faint; and to them that have no might he increaseth strength. . . . But they that wait upon the Lord shall renew their strength; they shall mount up with wings as eagles; they shall run and not be weary. . . ."

Yes, change your world. One of our founding fathers, Thomas Paine, said, "We have it within our power to begin the world over again." We can do it by doing together what no one church could do by itself. God bless you and thank you very much.